Yale Egyptological Studies 7

The Inscription of Queen Katimala at Semna: Textual Evidence for the Origins of the Napatan State

Yale Egyptological Studies

Yale Egyptological Studies 7

The Inscription of Queen Katimala at Semna

Textual Evidence for the Origins of the Napatan State

John Coleman Darnell

Yale Egyptological Studies 7

ISBN 0-9740025-3-4

Printed in the United States of America on acid-free paper.

Contents

Editor's Preface

This seventh volume of the *Yale Egyptological Studies* marks a change in the scope of the series. Two additional scholars have joined the editorial staff, Professor Bentley Layton, Yale University, and Professor Hans-Werner Fischer-Elfert, Universität Leipzig. Most of the previous volumes of *YES* presented the results of colloquia and seminars by visiting scholars at Yale University. Volumes five and six were unplanned but fortunate departures from the earlier pattern in presenting two exceptional Yale University undergraduate senior essays in revised form; as such deserving student works appear in the future, they may find a place in the series as well. Although the *Yale Egyptological Studies* have thus far been limited to products of students and scholars working and teaching at Yale University, we hope to broaden the scope of the series and widen the field of potential future publication. We invite submissions of scholarly monographs appropriate for the size and presentation of the series; potential topics would involve a chronological scope from the Predynastic through Coptic Periods, and themes ranging from history and archaeology to literature and philology.

John Coleman Darnell
New Haven, CT
November 20, 2005

Preface

Discussions of the history of Nubia during the first millennium bce and examinations of the origins of the Napatan state not infrequently refer to the inscription of Katimala, but of this inscription only two philological discussions of any depth have as yet appeared in print. The present study will probably neither add greatly to the debate over the chronological and political significance of the early Napatan royal burials in the much discussed el-Kurru cemetery, nor is it likely to end debate over the significance of the yet mysterious queen named Katimala. Even the proper reading of her name—Katimala or Karimala—remains uncertain (although, as discussed below, this may not in the end be such a problem). The investigation filling the following pages seeks to demonstrate at the very least, however, that Katimala's inscription is neither illegible, nor completely obscure. Palaeographically the text belongs to the time of the Twenty-First to Twenty-Second Dynasties in Egypt; grammatically the text is written in a good, epistolary Late Egyptian, nevertheless with a few added demotico-Copticisms, evincing a somewhat more colloquial and perhaps slightly later level of grammar than that common to the bulk of the Late Ramesside letters.

The text and iconography of Katimala's Semna tableau fit together to tell the story of an embattled Nubian realm, a disabled and despairing king and a militantly religious queen. These events appear to have occurred early during the roughly three centuries of seeming archaeological and epigraphic darkness that settle over Lower Nubia following the period of civil war that in Egypt troubles the reign of the last Ramesses. At some point during the Twenty-First Dynasty, when Egypt turned in upon herself, sharing power between a northern pharaoh and a high priest of Amun ruling the south, all the while looting the tombs of the great rulers of the glorious and only recently ended New Kingdom—while Egypt repaired the scars of political and military decay and economic collapse, and cannibalized the eschatological well-being of her own ancient dead—queen Katimala appears to have set Nubia on the road to political unity and military power, propelled by a personal and crusading devotion to the god Amun. After the depredations of the Amarna Period and the renewal of piety under the more successful Ramesside "doctrine" of the solar religion, during the Nineteenth and Twentieth Dynasties in Egypt, Nubia under Katimala became the home to a new and brashly militant Amunism.

The present work has had a long gestation of almost two decades, originating as a project while reading Napatan inscriptions with Klaus Baer in 1986, and beginning finally to attain its present shape while reading the text with my students in a class on Napatan Historical Inscriptions at Yale University during Fall Semester, 1999. The present edition of the text has profited greatly from comments by the students who participated in that class, Ms. Colleen Manassa and Ms. Cara Sargent (both now PhD's as well). My work on the Katimala inscription advanced further while reading and advising the doctoral dissertation of Ms. Sargent, an analysis of the grammar of the Napatan Historical Inscriptions (The Napatan Royal Inscriptions: Egyptian in Nubia, accepted Spring 2004, publication in preparation). During the Spring Semester of 2005, Ms. Sargent, having completed her dissertation, returned to Yale to help teach a course on those inscriptions, and I further benefited from renewed discussions with her, and from the comments of Mr. David Klotz and Mr. Marc Leblanc, the students in that more recent class. Dr. Hans-Werner Fischer-Elfert offered a number of helpful suggestions and references. Ms. Manassa provided considerable bibliographic assistance in the preparation of the present publication, and helped in preparing the glossary and plates, typing the hieroglyphic transcription, and in checking references. Susanne Wilhelm is responsible for the typesetting of the manuscript, and I would like to thank her for copyediting and the creation of a new format for *YES*.

While the following analysis of Katimala's inscription is not based on a collation of the text in Khartoum, Schliephack's excellent photographs and Caminos' own collated copy leave but few areas calling for further scrutiny. The Oriental Institute of the University of Chicago supplied copies of Schliephack's photographs at a reasonable price, and granted permission for their publication here. Dr. Patricia Spencer and the Egypt Exploration Society kindly granted permission to reproduce Caminos' drawings of the Katimala tableau.

The present publication will hopefully advance the study of Katimala's inscription, and provide a new document of no small literary merit to the evidence for the study of the early Third Intermediate Period in Nubia. Most of what has been written regarding Lower Nubia during the early first millennium bce has been speculative, and based on archaeological material; the present study itself remains speculative in its concluding interpretive sections, but now provides a more ample epigraphic element on which to base that speculation. Even as far as the proper reading of the inscription and interpretation of the iconography of the tableau, problems remain, but Katimala does at least emerge as a remarkable person, a worthy ancestor—though we may not perceive clearly the lines of connection—for her often equally remarkable successors of the Twenty-Fifth Dynasty.

John Coleman Darnell
New Haven, CT
February 18, 2005

List of Illustrations

FIGURES

PLATES

"After leaving Sarras the first serious obstacle to navigation is the cataract of Semneh, the foot of which is reached after an eleven miles pull against a smooth, swift current running between high rocky banks. Then come ten miles of broken, swifter flowing water, against which, however, with the help of a moderate breeze, it is possible to proceed without having recourse to the track lines. At the head of this rapid is the great 'Gate of Semneh,' a narrow gorge, between two rocky cliffs, partly blocked by two islands about equi-distant from the shores and from each other. Through the three passages thus formed, the whole pent up volume of the Nile rushes through a sluice gate. Here the boats have to be unloaded, and their cargoes, package by package, carried for half a mile over the rocks and depositied, near smooth water, above the cataract. Then the track lines are passed round the rocks and two or three boats' crews manning one line, each boat is in turn hauled by main force up the water slide and run in opposite its cargo on the beach."

Colvile, *History of the Sudan Campaign* 1, pp. 117–18

Introduction — Katimala's Tableau and Semna

The origins of the Napatan Kingdom, later to become, if but for a short time, the Napatan Empire of Kush and Egypt, remain mysterious. Perhaps the only known epigraphic document that might shed light on the birth of this Nubian state is the inscription of a queen Katimala at Semna. At some point, apparently during the early first millennium BCE, artisans carved a relatively large tableau and accompanying inscription on the southern façade of the Eighteenth Dynasty temple of Semna. Although the inscription is now published in both photograph and facsimile drawing, prior to the present study only two valiant attempts at translation and philological commentary have appeared. In spite of the almost total uncertainty that reigns in the Egyptological literature regarding the specific nature and import of the text, much commentary on the place and importance of Katimala continues to appear; most seem resigned to the perceived impossibility of understanding the inscription,[1] and may seek an explanation for the text's difficulty in some aspect of it's carving,[2] or even by suggesting that the author and commissioner were at best partially educated.[3] Given the general recognition of the importance of the text, and the apparent acceptance of its obscurity, the relatively recent publication of a facsimile of the inscription of Katimala at Kumma makes a fresh examination of the text desirable.[4]

---

[1] Compare Kendall, in Wenig, ed., *Studien zum antiken Sudan,* pp. 4 and 59–63, *et passim,* and Morkot, in Wenig, ed., *Studien zum antiken Sudan,* p. 145; Morkot's conclusion that the text "apparently refers to military activities, but beyond this little can be gleaned from it" is, as the present study hopes to show, fortunately too pessimistic, as is Kendall's inaccurate statement (p. 60) that "no connected translation is possible due to the carelessness with which the signs and words were carved." See also Lohwasser, *Die königlichen Frauen,* refs. p. 383 (on p. 16 she states that Katimala's inscription "ist zwar neuägyptisch, doch in vielen Passagen für uns nicht verständlich geschrieben").

[2] So Caminos, *Semna-Kumma* 1, p. 24: "The sheer clumsiness of the writing and the imperfect condition of the wall add greatly to the intrinsic difficulties and ambiguities of the text as such." Similarly, Török, *Kingdom of Kush,* p. 54, states that the preservation of Katimala's text is poor. On the whole these are inaccurate assessments.

[3] Although he acknowledges that the text is difficult and not yet fully understood, Török, *Birth of an Ancient African Kingdom,* p. 49 concludes that "the genre of the text is only partly monumental (dating and narrative portion) and gives the impression of a half-educated author and of a commissioner who was not aware of the Egyptian traditions of royal utterances and of the nature of king-deity interactions;" for him the text is the product of "poorly educated *literati.*"

[4] Bibliography: Porter and Moss, *Topographical Bibliography* VII, pp. 145–47; Grapow, *ZÄS* 76 (1940): 24–41; Reisner, Dunham, and Janssen, *Semna Kumma,* pls. 11 and 13–14; Pierce, in Eide,

The Semna inscription remains thus far the only evidence for the reign of Queen Katimala. Based on the palaeography and grammar of the inscriptions and the iconography of the images (all discussed in detail below), Katimala's tableau appears to date to the time of the Egyptian Twenty-First Dynasty, or perhaps even the early Twenty-Second Dynasty, that is to say from sometime around the middle of the eleventh to the middle to latter portion of the tenth centuries BCE. Katimala's name is thus unlikely to have filled the cartouche of the earliest of the royal ancestors on the stela of Aspelta, and she is equally unlikely to have been the occupant of the earliest royal burial at el-Kurru, both of those now anonymous royal ancestors of the Twenty-Fifth Dynasty apparently dating to some time during the ninth century BCE.[5] Fortunately, however, Katimala commissioned her tableau at Semna, and providentially it has survived virtually intact, for through it we glimpse, however darkly, a remarkable queen of the Early Napatan Period, a worthy ancestor for the pugnacious and pious Piye of the Twenty-Fifth Dynasty.

Location

The fortress of Semna, on the west bank of the Nile in roughly the middle of the Batn el-Hagar, overlooked—with its mate the fortress of Kumma on the east bank—a barrier of rock that almost blocked the flow of the Nile during the period of low water.[6] Originally forming an integral part of the great Second Cataract fortified area of the Middle Kingdom, an element in the Twelfth Dynasty's defense-in-depth of the southern borders of the pharaonic state, the fortress of Semna returned to Egyptian service during the New Kingdom, following the period of Kerman ascendancy during the Second Intermediate Period.[7] The fortress of Semna itself belongs to the tripartite fortifications of the southern end of the Second Cataract, constructions of Sesostris III, and perhaps already the conception of Sesostris II.[8] The temple on which Katimala left her inscription is a construction of Hatshepsut and Thutmosis III.

Hägg, Pierce, and Török, *Fontes Historiae Nubiorum* 1, pp. 35–41; photographs, facsimile drawing, references, and some commentary, but no attempt at full translation of the main inscription, in Caminos, *Semna-Kumma* I, pp. 20–27. See also Lohwasser, *Die königlichen Frauen,* pp. 158–59.

[5] See Priese, *ZÄS* 98 (1972): 23, for the genealogy going two generations beyond Alara; Welsby, *The Kingdom of Kush,* pp. 13–16.

[6] See the evocative description of the site in Caminos, *Semna-Kumma* I, p. 3 (and the aerial photograph *ibid.,* pl. 3). See also the description of the Semna Gate in Colvile, *History of the Sudan Campaign* 1, pp. 117–18 (quoted at the beginning of the present work); Gleichen, ed., *Anglo-Egyptian Sudan* 1, p. 24: "Here [Semna Rapid] a narrow ridge of gneiss forms an awkward barrier. At high Nile the river sweeps over it without perceptible diminution of width (430 yards), but at low Nile, the rocks are bare save for a narrow channel, 45 yards broad and 65 feet deep, formed by erosion." See also Hume, *Geology of Egypt* 2/1, pp. 46–47 and pls. 28–31.

[7] For the Middle Kingdom Second Cataract fortresses see Kemp, *Ancient Egypt,* pp. 172–78; Obsomer, *Sésostris Ier,* pp. 352–59 *et passim.* For Semna during the Second Intermediate Period, see Smith, *Askut,* pp. 132–34. On the purpose of the Second Cataract fortresses see also Williams, in Teeter and Larson, eds., *Gold of Praise,* pp. 435–53.

[8] See Obsomer, *Sésostris Ier,* pp. 337–38.

Katimala's inscription occupies a prominent place on the west side of the south façade of the Semna Temple, to the left of the main entrance of the north-south elongated sanctuary of the temple proper.[9] Although the columns of the main inscription depart increasingly from the true vertical at the bottom, leaning towards the left, and even considering the general lack of crispness to the carving of the hieroglyphs, the scene itself is well executed, and the surface whereon the tableau is carved required no inconsiderable amount of preparation. To quote Caminos' description of the tableau:[10]

> "It is obviously adventitious: to carve it, it was necessary to remove from the wall texts and figures that had been engraved there in the mid-Eighteenth and early Twentieth Dynasties, say between ca. 1480 and 1150 BCE. They were effaced with exceptional thoroughness...."

The text and scene do not appear to be the result of a single brief visit, but rather more likely betoken a stable presence at Semna during the time of the Egyptian Twenty-First Dynasty.[11] Nor does the tableau contain any indication that it is a boundary marker; the theme of triumph over a dangerous, impious, and recurrent enemy threat and address to a council of chiefs speaks more of restoration and consolidation.

Katimala's tableau is not alone in augmenting the original Eighteenth Dynasty decoration of the temple of Semna; the depiction and inscription of a Viceroy of Kush from the reign of Ramesses III occupies the same wall of the façade of Semna Temple as that to which Katimala added her tableau, together with an earlier record of an Eighteenth Dynasty Viceroy.[12] In location Katimala's inscription mirrors—albeit on a grander scale—the tableau of Pinudjem I to the left of the entrance to the Colonnade Hall of Luxor Temple, the execution of which also required the partial erasure of earlier decoration.[13] The façade of Semna Temple shares with the façade of Luxor Temple's Colonnade Hall, and the adjoining interior south face of the southeastern wall of the Ramesside court of Luxor Temple, an agglomeration of inscriptions supple-

---

[9] For a view of the location of the inscription through the south gate of the fortress, see Hinkel, *Exodus from Nubia,* 34th sheet of unnumbered plates following p. 48. For a description of the architecture of the temple, see Caminos, *Semna-Kumma* I, pp. 12–15.

[10] Caminos, in Berger, Clerc, and Grimal, eds., *Hommages à Jean Leclant* 2, pp. 73–74.

[11] Kendall, in Wenig, ed., *Studien zum antiken Sudan,* p. 63, is thus incorrect when he suggests that Katimala's tableau "does not appear to be the work of a patient scribe; it was a hasty work, done perhaps under supervision of soldiers in extremis but placed prominently in a temple dedicated to the ancient revered ancestors who had once maintained order here." Likewise his suggestion at the same time that the text is the record of the southern incursion of an Egyptian army is unlikely. Caminos, *Semna-Kumma* 1, p. 24, also suggested that the signs of the main inscription were "presumably cut in haste or at all events without any great care by rather uncouth hands".

[12] Caminos, *Semna-Kumma* I, pp. 31–33 and pls. 14 and 19 (Panel 5, Ramesside), and pp. 27–31 and pls. 14 and 18-19 (Panel 4, Eighteenth Dynasty).

[13] Epigraphic Survey, *Reliefs and Inscriptions at Luxor Temple* 2, pls. 199–200, and pp. 52–54; Peden, *Graffiti,* p. 273.

mentary to the original decoration of the temple.[14] The façade of the Colonnade Hall reveals additions stretching into the Graeco-Roman Period, suggesting that the area immediately to the left of the entrance when entering the structure was the object of particular "popular" worship and a place of votive inscriptional surcharging of the walls during the Third Intermediate Period and later.[15] A similar situation may have obtained at Semna Temple. The addition of the Katimala tableau to a portion of the façade already the object of official "plackards" during the Eighteenth and Twentieth Dynasties suggests a continuity in the activity at the temple.

History of Modern Interest in the Tableau:

The first modern visitors to publish a reference to Katimala's tableau were Waddington and Hanbury in 1822, reporting on their visit to Semna on January 30, 1821; although they gave no description of the specific elements thereof, they did recognize that Katimala's tableau was a later addition, carved over the earlier decoration of the temple.[16] The first traveler to give a more detailed decription, and the first to provide an at least partial reproduction of the Katimala tableau, was Frédéric Cailliaud, who published a drawing of a portion of the tableau in 1823.[17] The only detailed philological examination of the tableau before the present study was that of Hermann Grapow, published in *ZÄS* in 1940. In 1994 R.H. Pierce offered a transliteration and translation in *Fontes Historiae Nubiorum* 1, pp. 35–41, with some notes and a short commentary,

---

[14] For the Colonnade Hall façade see those published in The Epigraphic Survey, *Reliefs and Inscriptions at Luxor Temple* 2, pls. 199–207; for the wall of the Ramesside court, see the references in Porter and Moss, *Topographical Bibliography* 2, 2nd ed., p. 307. See also Peden, *Graffiti,* pp. 272–73.

[15] Compare the "Ptah Who Hears Prayers" within the south thickness of the passage through the Eastern High Gate at Medinet Habu—Epigraphic Survey, *Medinet Habu* 8, pl. 608. For the forward portions of Egyptian temples as places of popular worship, see the comments of Bell, *JNES* 44 (1985): 270–71 and 275; *idem,* in Shafer, ed., *Temples of Ancient Egypt,* pp. 135 and 163–72.

[16] Waddington and Hanbury, *Journal of a Visit,* p. 306: "In the front is a large hieroglyphical tablet, of a later date than the temple, more deeply cut than the figures, and at the expense of the feet of some of them, and the entire legs of one." Caminos, *Semna-Kumma* I, p. 27, provides an overview of the publication history of the Katimala tableau. He states, however, that Burckhardt published a brief reference to the scene in 1819, recording a March 19, 1813 visit, but in his description of Semna (Burckhardt, *Travels in Nubia,* pp. 81–88) Burckhardt does not describe the Katimala tableau, although he does make a few definite references to specific elements of the temple's decoration, including hieroglyphs, and a boat containing Osiris (he refers to the scenes of Sesostris III, wearing Jubilee robe, enthroned in shrine atop a barque—Caminos, *Semna-Kumma* I, pls. 50 and 57–58); of the decoration of the outer walls he notes simply (Burckhardt, *Travels in Nubia,* p. 104): "On the exterior wall of the temple I distinguished several figures of Mendes or the Egyptian Priapus." Apparently he refers to the ram-headed Khnum on the right side of the lintel of the door on the main façade of Semna Temple (Caminos, *Semna-Kumma* I, pl. 20), although the multiplicity of "Priapus" images suggests more the temple at Kumma (see Caminos, *Semna-Kumma* II, pls. 18–19, 24–25, 29, 31–32, 34–36, 38, 40–45, and 61–73).

[17] Frédéric Cailliaud, *Voyage à Méroé,* Atlas 2, pl. 27 (5).

although he makes clear (p. 39) that "the 'translation' offered here is best described as a set of glosses and guesses, for in fact I do not understand this text."

A new examination of the inscription reveals that Katimala's account is an even more informative document than most appear to have supposed, and that Katimala was apparently a more remarkable woman than any may have thought. A proper reading of the text reveals that Katimala assumed sole rule of the Napatan realm from a male ruler, perhaps her own husband, after what may have been the former ruler's defeat at the hands of a rapacious enemy. The text relates that the male ruler became physically disabled, possibly after some skirmish with the inimical forces assailing the nascent Napatan realm. Although he may in fact have been victorious in the encounter, the text appears to emphasize that the enemy has brought repeated misery to the realm, and escaped again from the latest encounter. Katimala avers that she, with the help of Amun, then triumphed. A reference to the forefathers who once frightened their enemies, and who apparently thereby dwelt happily with their wives, hints strongly at some marital discord between Katimala and her less successful husband, assuming the king in question to be her husband and not her father.

The Scene and Annotations

The Scene

The left portion of the scene that occupies much of Katimala's tableau at Semna depicts Katimala, with a smaller female figure following close behind, facing to the right. Opposite them in the right portion of the scene stands the goddess Isis, facing left, two offering stands separating her divine figure from that of the queen. The columns of the main inscription are to the right of the goddess. Nine lines of text accompany the depictions within the scene, labeling the figures of the goddess and the queen.

The goddess Isis is a prominent element of the scene, although her name does not appear in the main inscription; conversely Amun, the deity with whom the text of the main inscription is so concerned, appears nowhere in the scene or its annotations. Isis appears but once in the surviving Thutmoside decoration of the temple,[18] and Semna would not seem to have been the site of an Iseum prior to the end of the New Kingdom.[19] Considering the content of the main inscription, the goddess Isis of Katimala's tableau is apparently Isis in her later well-established role as a goddess of war,[20] and the growth of an Isis cult at Semna is no more surprising than the slightly earlier rise of the cult of Isis at Giza.[21] By the Meroitic Period, images or intermediaries of the deities Amun and Isis may have acknowledged the proper ruler in rituals associated with the coronation journey of the southern ruler.[22]

The texts above both the goddess and the queen express clearly that the bouquets atop the offering stands—though the largest flowers may point toward the figure of the queen—belongs to the goddess Isis. The somewhat unexpected orientation of the two blooming flowers and one of the buds toward the figure of the queen[23] may in fact be the result of the constraints of limited space; if the composer of the tableau wished to allow the maximum space to the main inscription and the greatest possible

---

[18] Isis appears in the scene of the induction of the king into the temple on the north end of the east exterior wall—see Caminos, *Semna-Kumma* I, pl. 29.

[19] Compare the list of cult sites in Münster, *Untersuchungen zur Göttin Isis,* pp. 176–80.

[20] Compare Zabkar, *Hymns to Isis,* pp. 55–75.

[21] Zivie-Coche, *Giza au premier millénaire,* pp. 38–42.

[22] See Lohwasser, in Arnst, Hafemann, and Lohwasser, eds., *Begegnungen,* p. 293.

[23] As Caminos, *Buhen* I, p. 88 n. 3, notes, "the stem always hangs on the side of the offerer. Two exceptions to this rule are to be found in Queen Katimala's relief at Semna, but then her record is outlandish and bizarre on several counts."

stature to the figures of Isis and Katimala, then the available space between the goddess and the queen would not allow for the offering tables to be shifted farther toward the queen—so as to allow the flowers to point in the direction of the goddess—without the more voluminous robes of the queen obscuring a considerable portion of the offering table nearest the queen. Similar to the seeming disjunction in the significance of deities between text and scene is the absence of any depiction of a male ruler, although such a ruler seems to speak in the first two lines of the main inscription (see below).

The figure of the queen is reasonably svelte, somewhat evocative—as Caminos observed—of the figure of Nefertari at Abu Simbel, and just as far removed from the steatopygous physiognomies of a number of Meroitic depictions of royal women.[24] At the same time, however, the figure of Katimala is not dissimilar to the figure of Queen Abalo, the mother of Taharqa.[25] The figures of Katimala and the small figure behind her are proportionally of six heads in height; Isis as well may have belonged to the same canon of proportions, although her neck is slightly longer, suggesting she may have had a smaller head and have been an overall seven heads in height.[26] Katimala wears the vulture crown atop what appears to be her natural hair, worn close-cropped. This is not typical Egyptian regal fashion, in which the vulture crown is worn atop a long wig; there are, however, a number of Napatan and Meroitic parallels to this style.[27] She holds in her left hand a flail-like object, which Caminos identified as a queenly flywhisk;[28] in her right hand is what appears to be a small *ḥts*-scepter.[29] Two ribbons depend from the back of her head, apparently attached to the vulture crown. Her clothing consists of a tight fitting under dress ending at the ankles, with a more voluminous outer robe touching the ground, with sleeves stretching to the elbows; both are depicted as though diaphanous. As jewellery she wears a broad collar, and an armlet on the left upper arm.[30]

---

[24] Caminos, in Berger, Clerc, and Grimal, eds., *Hommages à Jean Leclant* 2, pp. 78–80; *idem, Semna-Kumma* 1, pp. 26–27; Pierce, in Eide, Hägg, Pierce, and Török, *Fontes Historiae Nubiorum* 1, p. 40.

[25] Compare Macadam, *Kawa* 1, pls. 9 and 10; for Queen Abalo see Lohwasser, *Die königlichen Frauen,* pp. 141–43.

[26] For Napatan-Meroitic canons of proportions, see conveniently Pomerantseva, in Welsby, ed., *Recent Research in Kushite History and Archaeology,* pp. 277–84. A reconstruction of the horns and solar disk of the goddess further supports the conclusion that her head was smaller than that of Katimala, and her figure of seven heads in height, an early version of the attenuated goddesses of later Nubian art.

[27] See Lohwasser, *Die königlichen Frauen,* pp. 219–20. Close parallels for the vulture crown, with well delineated wing and twin feathers, appear in images of the queens Irtitu and Cherisis (*ibid.,* p. 221, fig. 18, f and g). Katimala's crown appears to foreshadow type BXIX of Török, *The Royal Crowns of Kush,* pp. 24–25, with the addition of the vulture crown.

[28] Caminos, *Semna-Kumma* 1, p. 21, with references n. 2.

[29] For the significance of the *ḥts*-scepter see the remarks of Troy, *Patterns of Queenship,* pp. 83–89.

[30] According to Pierce, in Eide, Hägg, Pierce, and Török, *Fontes Historiae Nubiorum* 1, p. 39, the queen and the smaller figure following behind her are wearing ear pendants of what he terms a steloform type, but these do not appear in Caminos' epigraphic copy of the scene. Such earrings indeed appear in the copy by Weidenbach in Grapow, *ZÄS* 76 (1940).

The small, female figure standing behind the queen has close-cropped hair, and wears a tight fitting sheath dress, ending just below the breast, with what appears to be a single, diagonal shoulder strap. Caminos suggested that the figure behind the queen, due to its small size relative to the images of Katimala and Isis, might represent a girl.[31] Although this is possible, the small figure behind the image of Katimala recalls perhaps more strongly the miniaturized images of the attendants of the high priest Amenhotep in the Karnak scenes of his rewarding by Ramesses IX.[32] The figure holds a triply folded scarf in her left hand, and what seems to be a mirror in her right hand.[33]

A scarf of the sort the diminutive female holds is associated with "les rites d'habillement, et d'autre part les cérémonies de l'Ouvertures de l'année et l'intronisation royale et divine;"[34] the scarf is linked to perfume, and was used during ceremonies requiring physical effort, although the object itself does not appear to have become sacred in its own right. The strap passing diagonally across the figure's chest may in fact be another such scarf, worn by the small female figure. Such "stoles" as the one Katimala's attendant holds (and the one she perhaps wears as well) are apparently the origins of the Isiac stoles of the Graeco-Roman Period.[35] The wearing of the scarf around the neck during strenuous work also suggests that the perfumed cloth may have been intended to mask any offensive odors of a sweating body—the scarf preserved the *odor suavitatis* of the cult.[36] The presence of the stole implies that the small female in the Katimala tableau is involved in the care of a sacred image.

---

[31] Török, *Birth of an Ancient African Kingdom,* pp. 48 and 99, has more specifically—and erroneously as the present discussion will reveal—assumed the small figure behind the queen to be a representation of a princess, upon which he has built a concept of "generational duality" for the Katimala tableau.

[32] Caminos, *Semna-Kumma* 1, p. 21. For the Karnak scene see Lefebvre, *Inscriptions concernant les grands prêtres,* pl. 2; Schwaller de Lubicz, *The Temples of Karnak,* pls. 376–77. Compare also the small female figure—"the king's beloved bodily daughter, the god's wife of Amun, lady of the Two Lands, Maatkare"—in the scene of Pinudjem I from the east side of the exterior north wall of the Colonnade Hall of Luxor Temple—Epigraphic Survey, *Reliefs and Inscriptions at Luxor Temple* 2, pls. 199–200, and the commentary pp. 52–54.

[33] For the simple mirror, of the sort the small female figure carries, in later Napatan and Meroitic examples, see Hofmann, in Altenmüller and Germer, eds., *Miscellanea Aegyptologica,* pp. 97–118, and note the citations there (*ibid.,* pp. 112–15) of depictions of mirrors in Meroitic tomb chapel scenes at Gebel Barkal and Begarawiya.

[34] See the study of Traunecker, *Cahiers de la Bibliothèque Copte* 3 (1986): 93–110; see also *idem, Coptos,* pp. 193–201. To Traunecker's one example of the ruler wearing the scarf, add four occurrences of Thutmosis III wearing the scarf while clothing the figure of Amun-Min in scenes in the Eighteenth Dynasty Temple of Medinet Habu (*PM* II/2 p. 471 [61] and p. 468 [43] and [44]; Epigraphic Survey publication, with commentary by the present author, forthcoming—note that the Ptolemaic over-painting of the exterior scenes did away with the Thutmoside scarf, suggesting that the apparent increased use of the object by clergy—bark carriers—may have contributed to a discontinuation of its already rare use as a pharaonic attribute). Two further occurrences of the scarf, worn by Sesostris I, appear in Petrie, *Koptos,* pl. 10, fig. 2. Note also the scarf(?) with pendant *ʿnḫs* (two rows) depending from the ends, in Jeffreys and Malek, *JEA* 74 (1988): 28, fig. 10.

[35] See Traunecker, *Cahiers de la Bibliothèque Copte* 3 (1986): 93–110. For the Isiac *palla contabulata,* see also Eingartner, *Isis und ihre Dienerinnen,* pp. 73ff.

[36] On incense, the olfactory aspects of epiphany, and the *odor suavitatis,* see Brashear and Bülow,

The fact that the figure behind that of Katimala brings a mirror before the goddess Isis is an important iconographic feature, and makes probable an identification of the female figure at the left end of the tableau as an early example of a *šms.t Mw.t*, a "devotée of Mut," a priestly function well attested in Late Period Egypt.[37] The mirror as an offering to Isis indicates a syncretism of Isis and Hathor, and is a means of pacifying the potentially angry solar goddess,[38] echoing perhaps the presence of the *sḥtp*-bouquet in Katimala's tableau. Although in the text accompanying her image in the Katimala tableau the goddess merely acknowledges her receipt of the queen's offering, scenes and texts of mirror offerings from Graeco-Roman temples indicate that the goddess' unspoken reward for the queen's offering in the Katimala tableau may have been universal domination, the goddess granting to the queen that which the cosmic eyes behold.[39]

The presence of these elements in the Katimala tableau are appropriate to a scene of the worship of the goddess Isis, and serve, with the texts, to focus attention on the image of the goddess. Just as the figures of the queen and the attending priestess face towards the goddess in the center of the tableau, so the columns of the main inscription read from right to left, leading the reader ultimately to contemplation of the figure of the goddess Isis. The text and tableau may honor Katimala, and it is with her that we are most concerned in our interest in the tableau, but it is the goddess Isis who is the ultimate object of Katimala's—and her tableau's—veneration.

The protective presence of the amuletic Goddess of the Eye of the Sun, hovering behind the image of the queen (see the discussion below), is an emblematic counterpart to the goddess Isis, perhaps even another image of that very deity.[40] The amuletic Eye may also, with the queen's vulture crown and the apparent *šms.t Mw.t* who follows behind her royal personage, serve to present the goddess Mut as the divinity of the left side of the scene, in apposition to the figure of Isis on the right.[41] The goddess Mut herself can be the Eye of Re,[42] and provides the proper Theban sheen to the glamour

---

Magica Varia, pp. 53–54; note also the comments of Meyer-Dietrich, *Nechet und Nil,* p. 46, n. 116 (regarding Hymn to the Nile IV, 3), and p. 112, n. 391 (regarding CT I 333a).

[37] See Munro, *ZÄS* 95 (1969): 92–109; Husson, *L'offrande du miroir,* p. 33; Müller, *LdÄ* 5 (1984): col. 1148 and n. 19—note her citation of Piehl, *Recueil de travaux* 3 (1882): 28, with the less specific allusion to *s.t nb(.t) šms(.t) ḥnw.t=s*, "every woman who follows her mistress." Naguib, *Le clergé féminin,* does not appear to discuss the title.

[38] Husson, *L'offrande du miroir,* pp. 250–53 and 255–56.

[39] *ibid.*, pp. 257–58.

[40] In the third scene on the mythological P. Louvre 3069 (papyrus of the Chantress of Amun Baumuternekhtou), Udjat eyes accompanying the oars of chapter 148 of the Book of the Dead are labelled as "Isis"—see Piankoff and Rambova, *Mythological Papyri,* pl. 13.

[41] For the goddesses Mut and Isis in Napatan contexts see Lohwasser, *Die königlichen Frauen,* pp. 308–11; for an overview of the same deities in later Meroitic religion see Hofmann, in Haase and Temporini, eds., *Aufstieg und Niedergang* II 18.5, pp. 2815–17 and 2827–32.

[42] See for instance Te Velde, in Shoske, ed., *Akten des vierten internationalen Ägyptologen Kongresses,* vol. 3, pp. 395–403; Naguib, *Le clergé féminin,* pp. 75, 220, and 231; Darnell, *SAK* 24 (1997): 45. The Chronicle of Osorkon, l. 53, refers to the flame of Mut as that which will overtake any who may transgress the inscription (Epigraphic Survey, *Bubastite Portal,* pl. 19, l. 53; see also Caminos, *The Chronicle of Prince Osorkon,* pp. 72–73).

of the goddess Isis, appropriate in a tableau in which the main inscription emphasizes the necessity and rewards of trusting in Amun. The scene presents a syncretism of the goddesses Isis, Mut, and Hathor, with Isis dominant.[43]

The offering of the *sḥtp*-bouquet, with the amuletic depiction of the Eye of the Sun in the desert lands hovering protectively above and behind the image of the queen, recalls a portion of the text of the Mut Ritual (the Voyage of the Libyan Goddess, P. Berlin 3014 + 3053 XVI 6-XVII 1):[44]

ḥtp.ti m Rꜣ-ḥsꜣ mi iḥy=s
swꜣḏ.n=f
        smw=s nb rd
        ḏr ir=tw n tꜣ Nb(.t)-Tꜣ.wy
                sḫn=s ḥr=f
                        iw=s ḥr ḫꜣs.t

She is contented with Rohesa as (with) her swamp.
That it has become green,
        is with all her plants having flourished,
        for one has acted toward the Lady of the Two Lands,
                such that she might settle there,
                        while she is (yet) in the desert.

Caminos included in his copy of Katimala's tableau a later image added to the scene, beneath the outstretched wing of the vulture goddess, and suggested that it might be of some antiquity.[45] The object most closely resembles an anchor, and from the design could be as early as Roman imperial times,[46] or as recent as the modern period.[47]

The style and iconography of the figures in Katimala's tableau suggest an early post-Ramesside date for the carving.[48] The text of the great inscription supports such a date as well, and allows some refinement thereof (see below).

---

43 For Mut and Isis, see Münster, *Untersuchungen zur Göttin Isis,* p. 146; for Isis and Hathor, *ibid.*, pp. 119–24; for Hathor and Mut, see Te Velde, *JEOL* 26 (1979/80): 7, and the present author's comments in Epigraphic Survey, *Reliefs and Inscriptions at Luxor Temple* 1, p. 31 n. f. Note also Brack and Brack, *Das Grab des Haremheb,* pp. 29–30, text 11c, in which the goddess Mut appears as the returning Hathoric goddess.

44 See conveniently Verhoeven and Derchain, *Le Voyage de la déesse libyque,* pl. L, l. 2, with pls. 5 and 8 (B XVI, 4–6; E 32–33).

45 Caminos, *Semna-Kumma* 1, pp. 21-22; he notes that although Cailliaud and Weidenbach omitted the image from their copies of the tableau, the object appears in Lepsius' paper squeeze. He notes that it is an image "vaguely resembling a grapnel: there is a ring attached to the top of a vertical shaft or pole having at the lower end two averted barb- or fluke-like projections."

46 Casson, *Ships and Seamanship,* pp. 252–55; Curryer, *Anchors,* pp. 24–32.

47 Anchors of the Islamic world have exhibited a variety of shapes (Hourani, *Arab Seafaring,* pp. 152–54), but this could in fact be late medieval or early modern (nineteenth century tourist *dahabiyahs* carried such anchors—compare that visible beneath the bowsprit of the boat in a photograph by Antonio Beato in Blottière, *Vintage Egypt,* pp. 178–79).

48 Török, *Birth of an Ancient African Kingdom,* p. 99, suggests that the texts and reliefs of the Osorkon II chapel at Karnak, PM II 15 (56), provided the template of Katimala titulary and rep-

The Annotations to the Scene

Text of Isis:

[1]ḏd<-mdw> in ꜣs.t mw.t nṯr ir.t [2]Rꜥ ḥnw.t nṯr.w nb.w
šsp(=i)[a] [3]sḥtp[b] n(y) ḥm.t-nsw.t wr.t sꜣ.t nsw.t [4]Kꜣ[[5]tymꜣlw mꜣꜥ.ti-ḫrw(?)]

Speech by Isis, mother of the god, the Eye of Re, mistress of all the gods: I am receiving the bouquet of the great wife of the king, Ka[timala, vindicated(?)].

Text above the Queen:

[6]ḥm.t-nsw.t wr.t sꜣ.t-nsw.t [6–7]Kꜣtymꜣlw[c] [7]mꜣꜥ.ti-ḫrw[d]
im(i) šsp[e] sḥtp(=i)

The great wife of the king, the daughter of the king, Katimala, vindicated: Do receive (my) bouquet.

Text in front of the Queen:

[8]nsw.t-bity[f] ḥm.t-nsw.t wr.t sꜣt nsw.t

The King of Upper and Lower Egypt, great wife of the king, daughter of the king.

Text behind the Queen:

[9]sꜣ n(y) ꜥnḫ ḥꜣ=s[g]

The protection of life surrounds her.

Text notes:

[a] The goddess' address to the queen begins with an initial *sḏm=f*, the dramatic *sḏm=f* "circumstantial" to the event depicted.

[b] The bouquet here receives the designation *sḥtp*, and Katimala's tableau thus clarifies the meaning of the term *sḥtp*, apparently otherwise occurring only in P. Harris I 37a, 11—see Grandet, *Le Papyrus Harris* I, vol. 2, p. 143, n. 591. As Grandet, *ibid.*, suggests, the term may be a variant of the *ḥtp*-bouquet (*ibid.*, p. 100, n. 410).

[c] Caminos believed the queen's name to be written clearly as Karimala in the annotation to the scene, as apparently Katimala within the text, although not impossibly

resentation; he further suggests that Katimala's titulary was modeled on that of Karoma B, wife of Osorkon II. He provides no specific arguments to support these suggestions, and they do not appear altogether convincing.

Karimala there also. Although he said he used Katimala more out of custom than conviction, Caminos nevertheless believed that the queen's name corresponded to Meroitic *Kdi-mel(ye)*.[49]

[d] The plant writing *m3ʿ-ḫrw*[50] does not necessarily indicate death,[51] although it may be an anticipation of a time in the future when the person will have died.[52]

[e] The imperative which the queen addresses to the goddess begins with the strengthening imperative *im(i)* of the verb *rḏi*, here not yet restricted to ϯ-causative verbs and Class V causative verbs as in Coptic.[53]

[f] Katimala has the title of *nsw.t-bity* in this short label.[54] If as interpreted here the queen assumes rule after the military defeat and physical collapse of a male ruler, an assumption of rule justified by her faith in Amun, then one would expect her to bear the title *nsw.t-bity* only here. When the yet living male ruler addresses her at the beginning of the main inscription, she would not yet have assumed the fullness of royal power at the time of her interview with the male ruler.

[g] The formula behind the queen is another example of the full writing of the protection formula with clearly written indirect genitive following *s3*.[55]

As no other monument now known appears to refer to this queen, even the proper reading of her name is somewhat in doubt. The queen's name could equally well be read as Karimala, and in fact, both readings—*K3tym3lw* and *K3rym3lw*—may support a single interpretation of the queen's name.[56] The initial element of her name is either the *k3ty* preferred here, or *k3ry*, in either transcription a possible occurrence of a "Meroitic" term that would appear to mean "woman."[57] The second element, apparently another

[49] Caminos, in Berger, Clerc, and Grimal, eds., *Hommages à Jean Leclant* 2, pp. 74–76.

[50] See Erichsen, *Acta Orientalia* 6, 272; Caminos, *JEA* 50 (1964): 89 n. 3; Gessler-Löhr, *GM* 116 (1990): 25–43.

[51] As Kendall, in Wenig, ed., *Studien zum antiken Sudan*, p. 60, assumed.

[52] See Jansen-Winkeln, *Ägyptische Biographien der 22. und 23. Dynastie* 1, p. 55, n. 45; Kruchten, *Le grand texte oraculaire de Djéhoutymose*, pp. 65–66; Winand, *Karnak* 11 (Paris, 2003), p. 640 n. e (note also Žaba, *Rock Inscriptions of Lower Nubia*, p. 152, on *wḥm ʿnḫ* in Nubian rock inscriptions).

[53] Wb. I 77, 8; Erman, *Neuaegyptische Grammatik*, p. 168, §356; Spiegelberg, *Demotische Grammatik*, pp. 99 and 256 (§216); Layton, *Coptic Grammar*, pp. 293–94, §367.

[54] Zibelius-Chen, in Gundlach, Kropp, and Leibundgut, eds., *Der Sudan in Vergangenheit und Gegenwart*, pp. 206–8, has previously discussed the possible implications.

[55] Compare the remarks of Clère, *RdÉ* 17 (1965): 206.

[56] As Caminos, *Semna-Kumma* 1, p. 23, remarks, the name of the queen may be read as *K3rym3lw* in the surviving version of her name in the annotations to the scene, and as *K3tym3lw* in the first line of the main inscription.

[57] The difficulty in choosing between the possible readings "Kati-" and "Kari-" for the initial element of the queen's name is perhaps not ultimately so significant as one might initially believe. The initial element, perhaps Meroitic *kədi*, may correspond to a Nubian term *karre* (see Bechhaus-Gerst, *SUGIA—Sprache und Geschichte in Afrika* 6 (1984/85): 94. A reading of the queen's name as Karimala would suggest a "Nubianized" Meroitic name.

"Meroitic" term *mꜣlw*, probably means "good," corresponds to Egyptian *nfr*, and appears as a personal name element as early as the Eighteenth Dynasty.[58] The queen's name may find a Meroitic version in the *Kdimlē(ye)* in a Meroitic text carved on the temple of Kalabsha.[59] That she is not of Meroitic date, however, is generally recognized.[60]

Grapow appears to have left the text behind the queen out of his consideration of the inscriptions. Kendall suggests interpreting the Udjat-eye as a representation of the goddess of the Eye of the Sun, reading the image as "the sign 'Eye' preceded by the words *sꜣ ḫꜣs.t* ('[Magical] protection of the foreign land')."[61] This suggestion ignores the fact that *sꜣ* is almost certainly an element in the formula of protection: *sꜣ n(y) ꜥnḫ ḥꜣ=s*. If *sꜣ* indeed is part of this formula, then *sꜣ* + Udjat-eye and associated signs *n(y) ꜥnḫ ḥꜣ=s* is a single inscription. From this follows the possibility that the Udjat-eye atop the small *ḫꜣs.t*-sign, all over the *nb*-basket, represents a direct genitive with *sꜣ*, a specification of the origin of the protection, and thus a designation of the deity from whom proceeds the protection (compare *Wb.* III 414, 18). The "heraldic" group of eye, foreign land sign, and basket together appear to represent in spare yet redolent symbolism the so-called Myth of the Solar Eye,[62] and this deity may be the *ir.t-Rꜥ*, the Eye of Re, or a more specific embodiment as Sekhmet or Tefnut.

The additions to the Udjat-eye in the scene accompanying the inscription of Katimala are in the style of additions to actual Udjat-eye amulets of the so-called Third Intermediate Period, and both the *ḫꜣs.t*-sign and the *nb*-basket appear on such "annotated" Udjat-eye amulets.[63] This suggests that most probably and most simply

58 Hofmann, *SUGIA—Sprache und Geschichte in Afrika* 3 (1981): 7–15.

59 For a discussion of the reading of the name in the tableau, and the possible Merotic parallel, with discussion of the possible meaning of that name, see Caminos, *Semna-Kumma* 1, pp. 23-26 (but without reference to the studies of Bechhaus-Gerst and Hofmann cited in the two preceeding notes).

60 According to Caminos, *Semna-Kumma* 1, p. 27, Katimala's tableau "dates back to the eighth or seventh century BC." Török, *Kingdom of Kush,* p. 40, dates her to the second half of the eighth century BCE; on p. 83 he more generally remarks that she appears to have reigned before Piye; he gives a similar dating on p. 127.

61 Kendall, in Wenig, ed., *Studien zum antiken Sudan,* p. 63.

62 Compare the brief summary of the concept, with some references, in Smith, in Helck and Westendorf, eds., *Lexikon der Ägyptologie* 5, cols. 1082–87; see also Derchain, *Les Monuments religieux à l'entrée de l'Ouady Helal;* Verhoeven and Derchain, *Le Voyage de la déesse libyque.* Kendall, in Wenig, ed., *Studien zum antiken Sudan,* p. 63, suggests that "Just as the 'Eye' dispelled the chaos and protected the sun god's domain in mythical times, so the queen, as her present counterpart, would have been given authority over Nubia as 'viceroy of Kush' in order to dispel with her magical powers the historical turmoil of the 'rebel' tribes, which threatened the well-being of Amun's cult." This imaginative politico-religious explanation of Katimala's role does not, however, account for the location of the Udjat-eye. The *wḏꜣ.t* can of course represent both the solar and lunar eyes of the cosmic deity (compare the references in Darnell, *SAK* 24 [1997]: 35–48); possibly, though less likely, the *wḏꜣ.t* with small *ḫꜣs.t*-sign here might in fact represent the lunar eye atop the horizon (compare Colin and Labrique, in Labrique, ed., *Religions méditerranéennes et orientales de l'antiquité,* pp. 45–78).

63 For an Udjat-eye atop a *ḫꜣs.t*-sign see Petrie, *Amulets,* pl. 25, fig. 141l (and p. 34), and Müller-Winkler, *Die ägyptischen Objekt-Amulette,* p. 102; for the basket compare Andrews, *Amulets of Ancient Egypt,* fig. 46, upper right; for elements such as the *ḫꜣs.t*-sign alluding to the story of the

the Udjat-eye in the Katimala tableau is a representation of an actual amulet as determinative of *sꜣ*, "protection," the amulet in question.[64] Though probably not to be read as part of the simple formula of protection,[65] the elaborate determinative of *sꜣ*-protection nevertheless imparts to the reader the story of the far wandering goddess of the Eye of the Sun. This association may ultimately have led to an association of the goddess of the Eye of the Sun with Katimala herself, an association of queen and Tefnut attested in later queenly iconography in Egypt.[66]

---

wandering goddess, compare the two apes *ibid.*, fig. 46, lower right. For these Udjat-eye combinations as particularly prevalent on amulets of Third Intermediate Period date, see Müller-Winkler, *Die ägyptischen Objekt-Amulette,* pp. 126–51. The Udjat-eye atop the basket also appears as a two-dimensional amuletic group—compare Feucht, *Das Grab des Nefersecheru,* pl. 21.

64 Compare *Wb.* III 415, 12-17; Ritner, *Mechanics of Ancient Egyptian Magical Practice,* pp. 49 and 51. Note also the use of the more general term *wḏꜣ*, "amulet," of *Wb.* I 401, 10, in l. 8 of the Chronicle of Osorkon, with specific determinative showing these to be "amuletic pectorals"—see Epigraphic Survey, *Bubasite Portal,* pl. 22; Caminos, *Chronicle,* p. 125 and p. 128, n. m.

65 Although a less likely alternative, the possibility remains that Katimala's tableau may have reinterpreted the formula of protection as *sꜣ nb n(y) ꜥnḫ ḥꜣ=s*, "all the protection of life surrounds her."

66 See Quaegebeur, in Maehler and Strocka, *Das ptolemäische Ägypten,* p. 251, n. 33.

The Main Inscription

Part 1: Introduction—the complaint of a ruler to Katimala:

Transliteration:

[1]ḥsb.t [a] *14 <ꜣbd> 2*[b] *pr.t sw 9*
ḏd ỉn[c] *ḥm=f n*[d] *ḥm.t nsw.t wr.t sꜣ.t nsw.t Kꜣtimꜣlw mꜣꜥ.tỉ-ḫrw*[e]

twnn <r> tnw[f]
ỉw bn twnn bꜣky[g] *m-ẖnw nꜣ bꜣk.w n ỉmn*
ỉw wn [2]ḫfty[h]
ỉw mn dỉ(=i) ḫpr[i] *tꜣ md.t n tꜣ rnp.t*[j] *ỉḫpr r=n* (or *r tꜣ=n?*)[k]
ỉw mn dỉ(=i) ḫpr=s[l] *ỉrr=w b(i)n*[m]
ỉw mn dỉ(=i) ḫpr n=n
ỉw wn wr
ỉw ꜥw(ꜣi)=f nbw ḥḏ[n]
mtw=f ỉr ỉmn n ⸢wꜥꜣ⸣[o] *[3]ṯny*[p] *im=i*[q]
ḫfty ⸢rwi⸣[r]

Translation:

[1]Year 14, <month> 2 of the Peret Season, day 9:
Speech by his majesty to the king's great wife and the daughter of the king,
Katimala, vindicated :

"Whither are we (to turn)
if we do not serve among the servants of Amun
when there is an [2]opponent?
otherwise will occur the annual thing that occurs to us;
otherwise it will go badly for them
(scil. the servants of Amun);
otherwise (it) will happen to us;
when there is a chieftain
who has robbed gold and silver,
and always treated Amun as ⸢accursed⸣—[3]who exaulted me.
The enemy ⸢escaped.⸣"

TEXT NOTES:

[a] The base on the *rnp.t*-sign recalls similar forms in the inscriptions of the Portal of Euergetes at the Khonsu Temple, Karnak.[67]

[b] Apparently the crescent of "month" was omitted.[68]

[c] The *sḏm.in=f* would be unexpected here, although it does occur most commonly with the verb *ḏd* with nominal subject,[69] and that subject is most commonly *ḥm=f* in Classical Egyptian Napatan texts.[70] The apparent *ḏd.in* may simply write *ḏd.n*.[71] Katimala might, however, allude to the use of *sḏm.in* in headings of legal documents,[72] a means of introducing an important nominal subject.[73] See also above, p. 12.

[d] A number of possible solutions suggest themselves to explain what follows the apparent *ḏd.in* for *ḏd.n*. Following *ḥm* the text may have *f* for *s*,[74] with the following *n* for *m*. Alternatively one could assume the *f* in Katimala's inscription to be otiose, a result of the common group *ḥm=f* being mechanically copied here. Although a confusion of gender might exist here, the more straightforward solution is probably the better. A king speaks to Katimala at the outset,[75] and uses the first person plural pronoun. Then begins the speech of Katimala, although the exact boundary between the two speeches is less than clear. Such an understanding allows one to comprehend and clarify the opening of column 4—the one whom the fathers had accepted as successor

---

67 See Le Saout, in Traunecker, Le Saout, and Masson, *La Chapelle d'Achôris*, p. 176 and 236 (particularly nos. 939 and 944).

68 Grapow, *ZÄS* 76 (1940): 29, suggested that the date might be first month of *Pr.t*, the regnal year date including the two strokes alongside the *pr*-sign, citing the Amarna boundary stela S; his copy was, however, inaccurate—see Murnane and Van Siclen, *Boundary Stelae*, pp. 84–98.

69 Compare Winand, *Études de néo-égyptien* 1, p. 190 (§313), and Hintze, *Untersuchungen zu Stil und Sprache neuägyptischer Erzählungen* 1, p. 31 (both cited in Sargent, *Napatan Royal Inscriptions*, p. 64).

70 See Sargent, *Napatan Royal Inscriptions*, pp. 64–65.

71 Compare *ibid.*, pp. 29–30 and 65. If the inscription writes *ḏd.in* for *ḏd.n*, the inscription could be said to begin like a Ramesside legal deposition—compare Donker Van Heel and Haring, *Writing in a Workmen's Village*, pp. 170–71, 173–75, and 187–88.

72 See Sweeney, *Correspondence and Dialogue*, p. 151, n. 6, and note the occurrence of *ḏd.in* in legal terminology, for which see Černý and Groll, *Late Egyptian Grammar*, pp. 452–53 (ch. 44).

73 Compare Lustman, *Étude grammaticale du papyrus Bremner-Rhind*, p. 147, citing Winand, *Études de néo-égyptien* 1, p. 191, and Jansen-Winkeln, *Spätmittelägyptische Grammatik*, p. 329, §524.

74 For the viper for *s* see Fairman, *JEA* 36 (1950): 110–11; Derchain, *Le sacrifice de l'oryx*, p. 17 n. 6 (from p. 16); Epigraphic Survey, *The Temple of Khonsu* 1, commentary p. 26 n. c [to pl. 51]); see also Fairman, *ZÄS* 91 (1964): 8. An *s* and *f* interchange occurs in otherwise identical doorjamb texts in Epigraphic Survey, *The Temple of Khonsu* 2, pl. 193, A l. 3 (*im=f*), and B l. 3 (*im=s*). Borghouts, *The Magical Texts of Papyrus Leiden I 348*, p. 193 n. 1, suggests a derivation of the value *s* for the horned viper from its use a determinative for a word *s3*.

75 So Pierce, in Eide, Hägg, Pierce, and Török, *Fontes Historiae Nubiorum* 1, p. 36; Kendall, Wenig, ed., *Studien zum antiken Sudan*, p. 60, Lohwasser, *Die königlichen Frauen*, p. 159.

hastened to Katimala after having failed, apparently in his struggles with the enemy. The inscription thus begins with the speech of a male ruler to Katimala, who appears to be obsessed with the recurrence of an annual event that brings ill; the inscription then relates how as a result of Katimala not remembering the event of the year, that is, as a result of her not dwelling on failure, she succeeded where the male ruler apparently had not. The opening quotation clearly contains rather bitter memories of what has happened, and thus cannot belong to Katimala, on the basis of what she says later in her inscription. In a sense Katimala's inscription is a sort of *Königsnovelle,* beginning with a report of military disaster—or at least stalemate—providing the background, not unlike the old *ỉw=tw* formula (see below); the reference in l. 4 to a ruler hastening (*sin*) to the queen may in fact be an allusion to the time when the king made the statement with which the section begins.

[e] For the designation of the queen as "vindicated" see above, p. 13.

[f] The statement begins with the question *twnn* <*r*> *ṯnw*, "where shall we go?" with *r* omitted, a first present with adverbial predicate;[76] this is followed by the circumstantial negative first present. The context is apparently similar to that of P. Anastasi IV 10, 11–12,[77] in which the writer asks the man he accuses of illegally commandeering the services of Tjukten scouts: *iw=k r tnw iw=k r pr nym*, "Where will you (go); to whose house will you go?" The enemies of Egypt themselves, in self-accusation, may ask the same: *iw=n r twn*, "Where shall we go?".[78] The accusatory connotations of the question suggest self-doubt, perhaps even recognition by the unnamed ruler that a lack of faith in Amun may have contributed to his discomfiture.[79]

[g] The double reed leaves of *bꜣky* probably derive from the *w*-coil that can appear with *bꜣk*.[80] For the determinative of the verb *bꜣk* compare ll. 28–29 of the Dream Stela of Tanutamun.[81]

[h] The orthography *ḫf*<*ty*> is an attested "Late Egyptian" orthography of the word.[82] The mention of some opponent, an unnamed enemy, occurs as circumstantial *ỉw wn ḫfty*, the non-specific enemy of the adverbial predicate in the present tense in-

[76] Compare *Wb.* V 373, 14; Caminos, *Late-Egyptian Miscellanies,* p. 178; Edgerton and Wilson, *Historical Records of Ramses III,* p. 31, n. 56a.

[77] Gardiner, *Late-Egyptian Miscellanies,* p. 46, ll. 8–9.

[78] Epigraphic Survey, *Medinet Habu* 1, pl. 28, l. 56.

[79] As a parallel for a royal text opening with a question—his second possible reading of the portion of Katimala's inscription in question—Grapow, *ZÄS* 76 (1940): 30, cites *Urk.* IV 27 (referring more specifically to *Urk.* IV 27, 8–12, ll. 6–7 of the stela of Ahmose for Tetisheri).

[80] See Sethe, *Verbum,* p. 114, §196; on the *-y/-w/-ty* interchange, see Fecht, *Wortakzent und Silbenstruktur,* p. 94, §172; for later writings of *-w* as *-y* compare *nmḥy* for *nmḥw*—Osing, *Die Nominalbildung,* pp. 176 and 686 n. 799.

[81] Grimal, *Quatre stèles napatéennes,* p. 14, l. 13, and p. 15, l. 2.

[82] As Grapow, *ZÄS* 76 (1940): 30, observed; see also Caminos, *Tale of Woe,* p. 5.

troduced by *wn* in good Late Egyptian fashion.[83] Based on its negative counterpart *mn*, this *wn* functions adjectivally.[84] The statement *ỉw wn ḫfty* recalls what one might term the negative counterpart to such a pronouncement, *nn <wn> ḫfty=k*, apparently the judgement of referees spoken to victorious fencers in annotations accompanying scenes of ritual combat during the Jubilee celebrations of Amenhotep III as they appear in scenes in the tomb of Kheruef.[85] The opponent is not defeated, the male ruler tells Katimala; the enemy remains on the field, he is yet a contender.

ⁱ Initially one might suppose the reference to an enemy to be followed by two virtual relatives. These would be two occurrences of *ỉw* + perfect active *sḏm=f*[86] followed by (*ḥr*) + infinitive of *rḏỉ* with a following non-initial prospective *sḏm=f*. Such a use of *mn* as a helping verb, similar to *ʿḥʿ* or *ḥmsi*[87] appears to be otherwise unattested, however (but see further below).[88] One might also suggest that *mn m-di* here functions simply as a marker of the negative finalis, an early example of the rare Coptic use of ⲘⲘⲞⲚⲦⲀ= as initial element of the negative finalis.[89] The orthographies of *mn m-di=* omitting the *m* of *m-di* occur already in Late Egyptian (compare *Wb.* II 59, 9). Analogy with the rare occurrences of the Coptic negative finalis with ⲘⲘⲞⲚⲦⲀ= suggests the presence of a subject following *mn m-di* (otherwise, with the verb *ḫpr*, one would expect the subject followed by the stative of *ḫpr*). Considering orthography and syntax, we most reasonably have here the first person singular suffix pronoun unwritten after *di*, the ⲦⲀⲢⲈϤⲤⲰⲦⲘ finalis.[90] The initial elements of the sections here in question appear to be the circumstantial marker *iw* followed by the negation ⲘⲘⲞⲚ,

---

[83] Černý and Groll, *Late Egyptian Grammar,* pp. 296 and 392–98; Layton, *Coptic Grammar,* p. 248 (§322); Winand, *CdE* 63 (1989): 166–71; compare also the Stela of Nestasen 18–20 and 35 (cited in Sargent, *Napatan Royal Inscriptions,* pp. 282–83). Green, *Orientalia* 45 (1976): 404, cites portions of the first two lines of Katimala's inscription, and erroneously suggests reading *iw wn* in each occurrence as a writing of *iwnꜣ*.

[84] Junge, *Late Egyptian Grammar,* p. 172.

[85] See Piccione, in Teeter and Larson, eds., *Gold of Praise,* p. 343, and the references cited there.

[86] Černý and Groll, *Late Egyptian Grammar,* p. 510, §54.4 [for *ỉw* + perfect active *sḏm=f* as the pluperfect see *ibid.,* pp. 570–71, §63.2.8 and the references *ibid.,* p. 571 n. 1].

[87] For which see the basic study by Kruchten, *Études de syntaxe néo-égyptienne.*

[88] A possible parallel in l. 9 of the enthronement inscription of Irike-Ammanote (Macadam, *Kawa* 1, pls. 17 and 22), suggested by Sargent, *Napatan Royal Inscriptions,* p. 222–23 with n. 546, on the basis of an earlier version of the present study of Katimala's inscription, is probably, as Sargent alternatively suggested, "the circumstantial converter, and the verb *rmnw* 'remove,' as ADP 17."

[89] See Crum, *Coptic Dictionary,* pp. 167b–168a; Crum, in Crum and White, *The Monastery of Epiphanius* 2, p. 255 n. 3 to no. 384; Sethe, *ZÄS* 57 (1920): 138; Wiesmann, *ZÄS* 62 (1927): 66; Westendorf, *KHwb,* p. 93, citing Till, *Koptische Grammatik* (4th ed.), p. 150, §295; for the negative ⲘⲘⲞⲚⲦⲀ= following the circumstantial converter, as here, compare Crum, in Crum and White, *Monastery of Epiphanius* 2, p. 234, no. 302 (with n. 5); this rare form apparently supplies the negative finalis otherwise missing from the literary language (compare Layton, *Coptic Grammar,* p. 283, §357).

[90] See Johnson, *Demotic Verbal System,* pp. 277–79.

corresponding to Coptic (ⲉ)ⲙⲙⲟⲛ.[91] In conclusion, the two sections represent the later (ⲉ)ⲙⲙⲟⲛ ⲧⲁⲣⲉϥϣⲱⲡⲉ, "otherwise it will occur."[92] Katimala appears to make use of both the negations *bn* and *mn*, as occurs in Ramesside Egyptian texts as well.[93] The negative *mn* appears only in the Late Egyptian Napatan texts, and within that subset, only in the Stela of Harsiotef.[94]

[j] Is the thing an actual event, or a reference to misfortune as the "thing of the year"? For "annual books" as things to be avoided, compare Edwards, *Oracular Amuletic Decrees,* p. 17 n. 54, etc.

[k] We appear to have *ḫpr* used here to refer to the occurrence of some evil fortune. For this one may compare the use of *ḫpr.t* as a reference to the state of Egypt in the Prophecy of Neferti,[95] the Complaints of Khakheperresoneb,[96] and the Wadi el-Ḥôl literary inscription.[97] The occurrence of *b*(*i*)*n* at the end of the second of the three ⲧⲁⲣⲉϥⲥⲱⲧⲙ passages (for *ḫpr bin* compare *Wb.* III 262, 12–13) appears to support this understanding of *ḫpr* in this section. Katimala's inscription provides several orthographies of the status pronominalis of the preposition *r=*/*rr=* and *irr* in column 2, *ir=* in column 6. The prothetic *yodh* preceding *ḫpr* would be expected for that triliteral verb with weakened final radical already by the time of the late Nineteenth Dynasty.[98]

[l] The third person feminine singular suffix pronoun *s* written as though it were *sw* is again an attested Late Egyptian writing,[99] entirely in keeping with the thus far pure Late Egyptian grammar.

---

91 Layton, *Coptic Grammar,* pp. 188 (§245) and 340–41 (§424); Till, *Koptische Grammatik* (4th ed.), pp. 204 (§408) and 224–25 (§460); Stern, *Koptische Grammatik,* pp. 387–88, §594; Crum, *Coptic Dictionary,* pp. 168a–169a.

92 For the use of the finalis following a rhetorical question, as here, see Layton, *Coptic Grammar,* pp. 284–85, §358.

93 Compare the remarks of Manassa, *Great Karnak Inscription of Merneptah,* p. 19.

94 Compare the remarks of Sargent, *Napatan Royal Inscriptions,* pp. 258 and 299. Green, *Orientalia* 45 (1976): 404, appears to read *Mnw* as a personal name(?), translating "when *Mnw* is not allowing us to exist."

95 Helck, ed., *Die Prophezeiung des Nfr.tj,* p. 18.

96 Gardiner, *The Admonitions of an Egyptian Sage,* l. 10.

97 Darnell, *Theban Desert Road Survey* 1, p. 113 n. *bb*. Compare also the impersonal use of ϣⲱⲡⲉ for "to befall," with third person feminine subject (Crum, *Coptic Dictionary,* p. 578a).

98 See Winand, *Études de néo-égyptien* 1, pp. 345–46 (§545), and the chart p. 364.

99 Cf. Erman, *Neuaegyptische Grammatik,* p. 34, §74; Černý and Groll, *Late Egyptian Grammar,* §2.4.1, citing (n. 44); Černý and Gardiner, *Hieratic Ostraca* 1, pl. 70, 1, recto l. 5; see also Jansen-Winkeln, *Spätmittelägyptische Grammatik,* p. 132, and note the writing *sw* for *s* in line 7 of the Excommunication Stela of Aspalta (Grimal, *Quatre stèles napatéennes,* p. 38, l. 14, and pls. 9a and 9).

m The apparent double negative *bn mn* is unlikely,[100] and appears in fact to be a slightly misplaced *b(i)n* belonging to the preceding phrase.[101] The final two *n*'s write the expected single *n* of the suffix pronoun (compare the reduplicated *n* of the pronominal preformative of the first present *twn*, and the probable *n* as *nn* in the *iḫpr.t r tꜣ=n* of col. 2).

n The final portions of the king's statement contain an effective choice of words—the verb *ʿwꜣi*, "to rob" (*Wb.* I 171, 3–12), here apparently written *ʿw(ꜣi)* (compare the damaged orthography *ʿwꜣ* at the bottom of col. 3),[102] describes the enemy's treatment of humanity. Interestingly, the term *ʿwꜣi*, "to rob, plunder," appears in a section of the Duties of the Vizier, in a context suggesting that the crime might have particular relevance to the governance of Nubia and Upper Egypt.[103]

o The continuative here expresses habitual activity following *iw wn*.[104] The adverbial *n* ⌈*wʿꜣ*⌉, "accursedly, blasphemously,"[105] describing the enemy's treatment of Amun, recalls the *m wʿ* of P. Brooklyn 47.218.135 col. 5/17.[106] The orthography of *wʿꜣ* in Katimala's inscription apparently began with either coil-*w* over ʿ-arm, or the ʿ-arm overlapping a quail chick. The lower bit of a line slanting slightly down to the left, above the left end of the tusk, suggests the presence of two slanting strokes, the entire orthography being *wʿy*.[107] The blasphemy of rebels appears in l. 87 of the Piye Stela[108] and in ll. 3–4 of the Enthronement Text of Anlamani.[109] The word here read *ʿwꜣi* could, however, be a writing of *diw* (see the top of col. 4), and the word at the end of the second column could be *biꜣ* instead of *wʿꜣ*, the passage thereby having another sense (see the discussion below of an alternate reading of this part of the inscription). The use of the conjunctive here may even relate a sense of outrage on the part of the narrator.[110]

---

[100] The apparent examples of *nn mn* in *Wb.* II 59, 10, and Erman, *Neuaegyptische Grammatik,* p. 403, §796, are in fact *(i)n mn*—see Černý and Groll, *Late Egyptian Grammar,* pp. 400 (exx. 1110, 1111, and 1112) and 402 (ex. 1120).

[101] For *bin* with medial *yodh* unwritten, compare *Wb.* I 442; already First Intermediate Period—Vandier, *Moʿalla,* p. 206 (§II ι 3) and p. 208 n. b.

[102] Compare demotic orthographies *ʿwy*—see Erichsen, *Demotisches Glossar,* p. 58. The word in Katimala's inscription is damaged, and may in fact have had double strokes representing a *-y* ending.

[103] See Van den Boorn, *Duties of the Vizier,* pp. 257–59.

[104] See Winand, *Lingua Aegyptia* 9 (2001): 302–7.

[105] *Wb.* I 279, 14–17; Baer, *Or.* 34 (1965): 428–38; Müller-Wollermann, *Vergehen und Strafen,* pp. 31–32; see also Ritner, *Mechanics of Ancient Egyptian Magical Practice,* pp. 46 and 50.

[106] Jasnow, *Late Period Wisdom Text,* figs. 10–11, with commentary p. 110.

[107] For the orthography *wʿy* compare the example in Gardiner, *Ramesside Administrative Documents,* p. 54, l. 17 (Turin Strike Papyrus, recto 2, 9); cited Lesko, *Late Egyptian Dictionary* 1, p. 106.

[108] Grimal, *Pi(ʿnkh)y,* p. 29*, ll. 17–18, and p. 110, n. 305.

[109] Macadam, *Kawa* 1, pp. 44–50 and pls. 15–16; see Sargent, *Napatan Royal Inscriptions,* p. 146, n. 171.

[110] For the sometimes subjective opinion of a narrator, see Winand, *Lingua Aegyptia* 9 (2001): 293–329.

p The beginning of col. 3 may be the most lexicographically perplexing segment of Katimala's inscription; Grapow, *ZÄS* 76 (1940): 31, concluded succinctly but unhelpfully: "Was 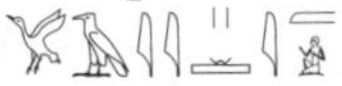 bedeuten soll, weiss ich nicht." One might take the short vertical in front of the bird to be the throw-stick for *ḳmꜣ*, with which the concluding reed-leafs would not be entirely incompatible. One might suggest the verb *pꜣ*, "to fly," a reference to the flight of the enemy,[111] in keeping with the image of the enemies of Egypt as small birds,[112] even sacrificial fowl.[113] The book-roll determinative does not support such a suggestion, however. Reading the sign G41 as *ṯni* provides a possible translation; reading the sign as *ḳmꜣ* or even *sḥw* does not yield a suitable meaning, but hieratic confusion is conceivable between G41 and G38 (here perhaps for *ḥtm*) or even G29 (*bꜣ*).[114] If one is in fact to read the word in question as *ṯni* then Katimala's inscription might recall the reference to the proper adherant of the ruler as the *ṯni*, "the elect," in the wisdom text on the Oxford writing board, ll. A2 and B4.[115] Certainly the term *ṯni* related more to private autobiography than to royal inscriptions, although it does appear in the later as well.[116]

One might read this as Katimala's call to the reader, or more properly in the context of the inscription her summons to the council to whom she later addresses herself:[117] "Exault me—the enemy has fled!" The *-y* ending of the word at the beginning of column 3 would suit an earlier orthography of the plural imperative, and the tiny stroke in front of the bird might in fact represent the Late Egyptian prothetic *yodh* of the imperative. The sense of *ṯni* and the parallels thereto speak against such an interpretation.

q The *ỉm=i* near the top of col. 3 apparently shows *m* introducing the direct object. While more common in even later stages of Egyptian, such appears already much earlier,[118] and is known of course for Late Egyptian.[119]

---

[111] Compare the souls of the enemy having "flown" in Epigraphic Survey, *Medinet Habu* 1, pl. 37, ll. 15–16; Epigraphic Survey, *Medinet Habu* 2, pl. 79, l. 10.

[112] Compare *Wb.* I 9, 8; Grapow, *Die bildlichen Ausdrücke,* p. 91.

[113] Junker, in Firchow, ed., *Ägyptologische Studien,* pp. 162–74; see also Darnell, in Mendel and Claudi, eds., *Ägypten im afro-orientalischen Kontext,* p. 91, n. 80.

[114] Less likely is a confusion with G14 (*nr*) or G21 (*nḥ*), although *nry im=i*, "respect me," would be an entirely reasonable initial summons by the queen.

[115] Barns, *JEA* 54 (1968): 71–76.

[116] See Rondot, *La Grande salle hypostyle de Karnak,* p. 76, n. b to No. 61, citing also Perdu, *RdÉ* 36 (1985): 105 n. f for private inscriptions, and Kitchen, *Ramesside Inscriptions* 2, p. 583, l. 11 and p. 604, l. 5 for royal monuments. For the latter, in a somewhat different context, see also Epigraphic Survey, *Reliefs and Inscriptions at Luxor Temple* 1, pp. 45–46, n. b to pl. 125, frags. 2125 + 2076b, l. 4. Note also Schade-Busch, *Zur Königsideologie Amenophis' III.,* p. 241 no. 146a (Khnum says *ṯni=i irw=f).*

[117] Compare the references to similar passages in Grandet, *Papyrus Harris I,* vol. 2, p. 215, n. 895.

[118] See Spiegelberg, *RdT* 26 (1904): 34–35; Silverman, *Or.* 49 (1980): 199–203; Loprieno, *Ancient Egyptian,* pp. 198–99; Černý, *Coptic Etymological Dictionary,* p. 102.

[119] Cf. Černý and Groll, *Late Egyptian Grammar,* p. 94, citing Černý, *Late Ramesside Letters,* p. 45, l. 14.

⸢ *ḫfty rwi* appears to conclude the king's report to Katimala, although the beginning of the latter's initial address is not marked (see below). The phrase, if it is a First Present as interpreted here, appears to treat *ḫfty*—although without preceding article—as a defined noun. The phrase *ḫfty rwi* is the first initial form after the king's opening *twnn r tnw*, and frames the king's pronouncement in initial forms. The initial form immediately following *ḫfty rwi* appears to open the queen's speech.

COMMENTARY:

Although the inscription opens—*hysteron proteron*—with what appears to be the speech of a king to Katimala (his wife?), we know from l. 4 that the opening of the event was the coming of the king to Katimala. A male ruler comes to a female ruler to make report of enemy activity in an elaboration of the old *iw=tw* formula. The bulk of the male ruler's pronouncement centers on three subordinate clauses built around the verb *ḫpr*. The occurrence of the event then reappears in the queen's speech, in which the female ruler states that the event did not occur because she did not dwell upon it (as we have seen the male ruler did). Her trust in Amun overriding the horrors of the seemingly endless cycle of events recalls a portion of the Teaching of Sasobek:[120] *ptr ny ḫpr.ny iw ḫpr=f k3p*(?) *imn sḫr.w nṯr*, "See, it cannot happen—it happens; concealed(?) and hidden are the plans of the deity." The frequent use of the verb *ḫpr* and its derivatives in the ruler's statement suggests an allusion to the pessimistic strain in discourses and teachings.[121]

Although the king refers to the worship of Amun, his question, and the queen's subsequent contrast of her faith in Amun with the situation that obtained earlier, together suggest that the worship of Amun may not have been so widespread and continuous, even amongst the Nubian elite, during the early post-Ramesside Period.[122] Alternatively, and perhaps more plausibly, the queen employs a literary *topos*—the trouble must have resulted from disobedience to Amun.[123] Just as Tutankhamun's Restoration Stela describes lack of military success as one of the results of the Amarna Period,[124] so Katimala appears to project back a possible ignoring of Amun and neglect of his cult to explain a period in which the forces of the burgeoning Napatan state appear not to have enjoyed success.

However, this important and difficult section of Katimala's inscription is subject to another, radically different interpretation. If the possible *b*(*i*)*n* in *iw mn di*(=*i*) *ḫpr=s irr=w b*(*i*)*n* is an orthography of the negative *bn*, the interpretation offered above becomes untenable. One might then suggest that *mn* in the first portion of

[120] P. Ramesseum I Bi 10–11 = Barns, *Five Ramesseum Papyri,* pl. 2.

[121] Compare the clusterings of *ḫpr* in the Teaching of Sasobek—see *ibid.*, glossary p. 39.

[122] Contra the assumption that Katimala's inscription implies the existence of the cult of Amun in Lower Nubia "as if it had been flourishing continuously and had never been disrupted until the time of writing" (Kendall, in Wenig, ed., *Studien zum antiken Sudan,* p. 61; Bennett, GM 173 [1999]: 7).

[123] For the "time of troubles *topos*," see Manassa, *Great Karnak Inscription of Merneptah,* pp. 110–13, and the references cited there.

[124] Helck, *Urkunden,* p. 2027, ll. 13–14 (ll. 8–9 of the stela).

Katimala's inscription is in all instances the verb "to remain, to continue," as the orthography with the sign Y5 alone would in fact suggest. Accepting this, one would seem to have *mn* (*r*/*ḥr*) + infinitive, "to continue/persist in doing" something, a use of *mn* parallel but unrelated to the more common auxiliary use of *ꜥḥꜥ*, *ḥmsi*, and *sḏr* in Late Egyptian.[125] Although a recognizable construction of *mn* + pseudoverbal construction does not appear to have existed as a common construction in Late Egyptian, Coptic examples of ⲙⲟⲩⲛ + following circumstantial do occur, for example: ⲁϥⲙⲟⲩⲛ ⲇⲉ ⲉⲃⲟⲗ ⲉϥϣⲗⲏⲗ,[126] ⲉⲩⲙⲏⲛ ⲉⲩⲣⲁϣⲉ, etc.[127] If one were to understand an auxiliary use of *mn* in this portion of the inscription, the text would read:

twnn <r> tnw
ỉw bn twnn bꜣky m-ẖnw nꜣ bꜣk.w n ỉmn
ỉw wn [2]*ḫfty(.w)*
ỉw mn=w (ḥr) dỉ(.t) ḫpr tꜣ md.t n tꜣ rnp.t ỉḫpr.t n=n
ỉw mn=w (ḥr) dỉ(.t) ḫpr=s ỉrr=w
ỉw bn mn=w (ḥr) dỉ(.t) ḫpr n=n

Whither are we (to turn)
if we do not serve among the servants of Amun?
when there are [2]enemies;
who continue causing to happen the annual thing that occurs to us;
and who continue to cause that it happen to themselves;
but they will not continue causing that (it) happen to us;

Understood in this way, the following *iw wn wr* would no longer necessarily be parallel to the *iw wn ḫfty(.w)*, but would seem, as a contrast, to detail the opposing actions of an apparently "righteous" *wr*-ruler. Reading *diw* and *biꜣ* as suggested in the text notes above in the appropriate places of the following portion of the text, one might suggest reading:

ỉw wn wr
ỉw diw=f nbw ḥḏ
mtw=f ỉr ỉmn n ⌜biꜣ⌝ ṯny im=i
ḫfty ⌜rwi⌝

for there is a chieftain,
who has given gold and silver,
and treated Amun marvelously[128]—who exaulted me—
and the enemy ⌜escaped.⌝"

[125] See Kruchten, *Études de syntaxe néo-égyptienne.*

[126] Layton, *Coptic Grammar,* §358e.

[127] Crum, *Coptic Dictionary,* p. 171b. In this connection note also Sargent, *Egyptian in Nubia,* part 1, ch. 3, n. 47, discussing the possibility that *ir=f n=f ꜥꜣb.t ꜥꜣ* in l. 11 of the Dream Stela of Tanutamun is a circumstantial form, based on a comparison with (*ḥr*) *ir.t n=f ꜥꜣb.t ꜥꜣ*.

[128] Compare Habachi, *BIFAO* 73 (1973): 122, n. 2 (*biꜣw* as "wonderful"). Alternatively, one might suggest reading *mtw=f ir <n> Imn n ⌜biꜣ⌝*, "and acted <for> Amun as a marvel"—compare l. 23 of Kawa VI (Macadam, *Kawa* 1, pls. 11–12, a portion of the text recording the covenant Alara made with Amun).

Although grammatically quite different from the solution proposed at the beginning of this section, the alternative reading still emphasizes a state of annual and mutually detrimental conflict between the "Proto-Napatans" and some group of enemies. The alternative reading would, however, have this section end with a statement contrasting the apparently proper behavior of an unnamed *wr* with that of the *ḫfty* enemies. Against the alternative reading is the then meaningless conclusion "and the enemy ⸢escaped.⸣"

The reference to blasphemy on the part of the enemy could simply refer to the robberies they are said to have carried out (ll. 2 and 3); as the conquest of these enemies appears to be synonymous with the making of a new land for Amun (l. 8), they were perhaps at best unacquainted with Amun, if not outwardly hostile to the deity. Perhaps more subtly the blasphemy may merely allude to their opposition to the "House of Katimala"—in l. 86 of his Victory Stela, Piye refers to the chiefs who opposed him south of Memphis simply as "the rebels who blasphemed the god."[129]

Part 2: The Queen Responds

TRANSLITERATION:

[3]*ỉry bꜣk n ỉmn p3 ỉrw=ỉ*[a]
ỉw bwpw=ỉ sḫꜣy[b] *tꜣ md.t ỉḫpr r=ỉ m tꜣ rnp.t*
m-ḏr hꜣnᶜ=ỉ n ỉmn
ỉꜣd[d] *ᶜwꜣ*[e] *nbw(?) ḥḏ*

pꜣ [4]*dỉw*[f] *n(ꜣ)y=ỉ ỉt.w ỉšsp=[i] n=w*[g] *sỉn n=ỉ*
m-ḫt wywy=f[h]
ỉw=ỉ ỉr=f[i] *m ḏw.w nbw*[j]

ḫr ỉ.ỉr=ỉ[k] *ᶜm*[l] *m tꜣ rnp.t*
ỉꜣy nḫt ḥkꜣy pꜣ nṯr[m]

TRANSLATION:

[3]"What I did was to act as servant of Amun.
for I did not remember the event which happened to me this year,
since I have trusted in Amun,
who attacks him who robbed [gold and] ⸢silver⸣.

[4]He whom my fathers—to whom [I] have succeeded—appointed hastened to me,
after he had failed/become physically disabled;
and I did it in the mountains of gold;

For it was that year I achieved the understanding—
then powerful is the magic of god.

[129] Grimal, *Pi(ᶜnkh)y*, p. 29*, pl. 9.

Text Notes:

[a] The quotation of the king's report concludes with the announcement that the enemy—presumably the evil enemy who had so impressed the king—had in the end escaped. Although the record of the initial report of the male ruler opens with the expected introductory formula,[130] Katimala's speech commences without introduction, save for the probable imperative at the top of l. 3. The queen then addresses us; the use of the pseudocleft *sḏm pw ỉr.n=f*[131] serves to stress Katimala's actions, in contrast to those of the failed ruler—from the outset she stresses the differences between her pious approach and the fruitless campaigning of the king who preceded her. An inscription of Taharqa from Karnak also employs *iri(=i?) n=k bꜣk*, the suffix pronoun referring to Amun.[132]

[b] The orthography of *sḫꜣy*, with sign F18 as determinative, is—as Grapow, *ZÄS* 76 (1940): 28, observed—indicative of an early Third Intermediate Period date. The use of *sḫꜣ*, "to bring to mind," does not mean that the queen involuntarily forgot the event, but rather that she refused to recall it to herself.[133]

[c] The queen employs the verb *hnn* to describe her adherence to the cult of Amun.[134] One would expect the first person singular dependent pronoun to be used reflexively here,[135] but Katimala's text dispenses with this. Reliance on Amun removes all thought for the event, just as for the earlier Samut, reliance on Mut prevented all thought for children and siblings.[136]

[d] For the use of *ỉꜣd*, note the epithet of Amun *pꜣ-wšb-ỉꜣd*.[137] Here we most likely have an allusion to this epithet, wherein Amun brings the troubles he normally relieves down upon the heads of the damned.

[e] The orthography of *ꜥwꜣ(i)*, though damaged, appears to have been *ꜥ*-arm and quail chick composite, followed by *ꜣ* (compare the clipped orthography *ꜥw(ꜣi)* near the end of col. 2).

---

[130] See Morschauser, in Goedicke, ed., *Perspectives on the Battle of Kadesh,* p. 135.

[131] The *sḏm pꜣ sḏm=f* of Groll, *Non-Verbal Sentence Patterns,* p. 70.

[132] Vernus, *BIFAO* 75 (1975): 51 n. f, and the references cited there (he also refers to Grapow's publication of the Katimala inscription).

[133] For the basic meaning of *sḫꜣ* compare Allen in Wiener and Allen, *JNES* 57 (1998): 15.

[134] For the orthography of *hnn* in Katimala's inscription, see *Wb.* II 494; Lesko, *Dictionary of Late Egyptian* 2, p. 83; and Osing, *Nominalbildung* 2, p. 803 (n. 1025). For other statements involving *hn* as trust in a deity, see Jansen-Winkeln, *Sentenzen,* pp. 104–5.

[135] See Lefebvre, *Inscriptions concernant les grands prêtres,* pp. 8–9; Kruchten, *Les annales des prêtres de Karnak,* p. 31.

[136] See Vernus, *RdÉ* 30 (1978): 135. Does Katimala perhaps imply some sort of more formal self dedication to Amun, in the mold of Samut's dedication to Mut?

[137] For which see Leclant, in Firchow, ed., *Ägyptologische Studien,* pp. 197–204; Vernus, in Vercoutter, ed., *Hommages à la mémoire de Serge Sauneron* 1, pp. 472–73, with n. 5.

[f] The nominalized relative *diw* is written as the arm with conical loaf overlapping the quail chick, a form deriving from earlier, Ramesside monumental orthography.[138] The prothetic *yodh*, which one might otherwise expect, is lacking following the definite article, in good Late Egyptian fashion.[139]

[g] The phrase occurs again in ll. 5–6. If a reading *iššp.n=w* were possible, one could understand a relative form standing in apposition to the preceding—"the one whom they have received," a reference to the deceased previous, male ruler—see *Wb.* IV 531, 11; a *sḏm.n=f* relative would, however, be an unexpected departure from otherwise good Late Egyptian forms in Katimala's inscription. Fortunately for the understanding of this passage, a strikingly similar use of *šsp* occurs in l. 15 of the inscription of the High Priest Amenhotep on the south side of the east exterior wall of the bark shrine of Thutmosis III between the Seventh and Eighth Pylons at Karnak Temple: *iššp=i n=w* ⌈*ḫr.t*⌉, "from whom I took over ⌈affairs⌉".[140] The absence of expressed object of *šsp* in Katimala's inscription is not disturbing (compare *Wb.* IV 533, 18); the understood object is probably *iꜣw.t*, "office."[141] The omission of such an object appears to have lead to the idiom *šsp n*, "to succeed to," literally "to receive through the agency of."[142]

[h] The word *wywy* in this passage (written as *wy sp-sn.nw*) is a variant orthography of the word *wiꜣwiꜣ*, a word that may refer to incompetent behavior, not necessarily to physical inability.[143] More specifically, *wiꜣwiꜣ* appears "to indicate rather a reluctance or an inability to fulfill one's duty than the actual fact of the neglect itself."[144] In the scene of festival combat beneath the window of appearances at Medinet Habu, an

---

138 Compare the remarks in Manassa, *Great Karnak Inscription of Merneptah,* p. 142, n. 42, and p. 144 (a form of the preterite *sḏm=f*); see also the comments of Fischer, *MMJ* 12 (1978): 15 with n. 122.

139 See the remarks of Winand, *Études de néo-égyptien* 1, p. 381 (§600) and 384 (§604).

140 See Wente, *JNES* 25 (1966): pl. 8 and fig. 2, with p. 80, n. 15a, assuming with Wente that the *ḫr* following *n=w* belongs to *ḫr.t*; if not, the parallel with Katimala's text is even more striking.

141 For the lack of expressed object of *šsp* note *Wb.* IV 533, 18; for the probable object *iꜣw.t* see *Wb.* IV 532, 10; Grandet, *Papyrus Harris I* 2, p. 236 n. 915; etc.

142 See Gardiner, *JEA* 27 (1941): 60–61 n. 7; *idem, Inscription of Mes,* pp. 18–19; Černý, in *Studies Griffith,* p. 53; Caminos, *Late-Egyptian Miscellanies,* p. 10.

143 *Wb.* I 272, 9-10; Wente, *Late Ramesside Letters,* p. 81, n. p; Meeks, *Année lexicographique* 2 (1978), no. 78.0888. So in P. 10463 verso 2–3 (Caminos, *JEA* 49 [1963]: pls. 6 and 6a, and notes p. 35) the Theban mayor Sennefer says that the man Baki is *wiwi*-lazy, elaborating this by adding: *mr=k wnm m sḏr*, "you loving to eat while lounging around" (note the use of *m* + infinitive for m *sḏr*, like *m ksw*, as if a verb of motion, rather than the stative). Note also the use of *wiꜣwiꜣ* to describe "ineptitude" (so Wente, *Letters from Ancient Egypt,* p. 51 [no. 57]). Sweeney, *Correspondence and Dialogue,* p. 207, ex. 42, translates *wiꜣwiꜣ* in O BM 50734+O. Gardiner 99+O. CGC 25673, recto 4 as "scandal," without further discussion.

144 Borghouts, in Demarée and Janssen, eds., *Gleanings from Deir el-Medîna,* p. 88 (and nn. 54–58, pp. 94–95). The concept of ineptitude for *wiꜣwiꜣ* is probably also behind the parallel statements *ḥḏ.wsy pr nb ḥr ns.t=k wiꜣwiꜣ.wsy ṯs.w=k*, "how damaging (or damaged?) is everything that comes forth on your tongue; how inept are your statements," in P. Anastasi I 28, 3 (Fischer-Elfert, *Die satirische Streitschrift, Textzusammenstellung* p. 155; see also the notes *idem, Die satirische Streitschrift, Übersetzung und Kommentar,* p. 239).

Egyptian tells a Nubian wrestling opponent that he is causing the Upper Nilotic foe to fall *wiꜣwiꜣ*, "helpless," before the king.[145] That passage suggests the *wiꜣwiꜣ* of the male ruler who addresses Katimala—his condition of *wiꜣwiꜣ* appears also to be the result of combat. The passage in Katimala's inscription seems to refer to a chosen male successor from whom the queen has taken over the ship of state. The *n* over the back of the *w*, but read before the bird, is a common placement in hieratic.

[i] The *ỉw=ỉ ỉr=f* is the sequential *ỉw=f ḥr sḏm* (understanding the objective [third] future would not allow for the fact that we know the enemy has already fled).[146]

[j] As Grapow, *ZÄS* 76 (1940): 33, recognized, Katimala's reference to the "mountains of gold" recalls the same toponym in the famous P. Turin 1879, 1899, and 1969 map of the gold-mining region[147] and in the text of the Kuban Stela.[148]

[k] The form *ḫr ỉir* here is not the predecessor of the demotic aorist, but rather *ḫr* + second tense.[149]

[l] The verb is apparently *ʿm* with the orthography *ʿmꜣm*, with the initial *ʿ* unwritten. There appears to be no *ʿ* in Meroitic, and the scribe of Katimala's inscription may simply have taken the orthography with the *ʿ*-arm as a writing of the causative ⲦⲀⲘⲞ. Note also the early attested interchange of *ʿ* with *ỉ* and *ỉꜣ*.[150]

[m] Grapow, *ZÄS* 76 (1940): 33, did indeed present "eine überraschende Parallele" for the statement that "powerful is the magic of god" from P. Turin Rossi and Pleyte 131, 6 (correcting Grapow's l. 7 to the correct l. 6 = Cat. 1993): *mk nḫt ḥkꜣy Ḥr r=ṯ*, "But, powerful is the magic of Horus against you."[151] The particle *iꜣy* here is not an interrogative, but rather is a marker indicating the attitude of the speaker, here in a didactic fashion,[152] introducing the inference the queen has made regarding divine power.

---

[145] Epigraphic Survey, *Medinet Habu* 2, pl. 111, 15; compare Edgerton and Wilson, *Historical Records of Ramses III,* p. 139 (translated "helpless"), and Wilson, *JEA* 17 (1931): 213 with n. 1.

[146] See Winand, *Études de néo-égyptien* 1, pp. 443–57 (§§689–708); Junge, *Late Egyptian Grammar,* pp. 207–12 (to his discussion and references, add also the discussion of *iw=f (ḥr) sḏm* inWente, review of Frandsen, *Outline of the Late Egyptian Verbal System,* in *JNES* 36 [1977]: 310–12).

[147] See Harrell, in Freidman, ed., *Egypt and Nubia,* pp. 239–40, and the references cited there; see also Gabolde, Galliano, et al., *Coptos,* p. 152.

[148] See Kitchen, *Ramesside Inscriptions* 2, pp. 353–60; Gabolde, Galliano, et al., *Coptos,* pp. 153 and 232 (cat. no. 113); Zibelius-Chen, in Berger, Clerc, and Grimal, eds., *Hommages à Jean Leclant* 2, pp. 411–17; see also the bibliography in Kitchen, *Ramesside Inscriptions. Translated and Annotated, Notes and Comments* 2, p. 214.

[149] See Johnson, *Demotic Verbal System,* pp. 142–44, and the references cited there; Neveu, *La particule* ꜥ*r en néo-égyptien,* pp. 57–59. For *ḫr* + *iir=f sḏm* indicating coordination and demarcation see Cassonnet, *Les temps seconds,* pp. 70–72.

[150] See Sethe, *Verbum* 1, p. 90, §148 (but note that the form *ỉꜣm* for *ʿm* for M. 511 appears in Sethe's edition, Pyr. 1417b, as *ʿm*; also, the bird in his *ỉꜣḳ* for T. 259 appears in Sethe's edition, Pyr. 312b, as the *ʿḳ* bird, although Sethe, *Übersetzung und Kommentar* 1, p. 377, still reads *ỉꜣḳ*).

[151] Rossi and Pleyte, *Papyrus de Turin,* pl. 131, l. 6.

[152] This contra Grapow, *ZÄS* 76 (1940): 34. Compare Černý and Groll, *Late Egyptian Grammar,* pp. 146–47; Layton, *Coptic Grammar,* §§ 238 (pp. 183–84) and 492 (pp. 399–400).

The text appears to indicate that a male ruler suffered defeat at the hands of the foe. Did he in fact receive fatal injuries in an encounter with the enemy (the state of *wywy*)? How one understands l. 4 has important implications for the proper understanding of the text as a whole. Is this male ruler who came before someone, this failed ruler, the same as the one who asks the apparently plaintive and perhaps even desperate question at the opening of the inscription? If so, then the remainder of the text is probably the speech of Katimala herself. Or do we have yet another, earlier male ruler here? Certainly the first person singular suffix pronouns of the inscriptions, when written, are those of the seated man. This in itself, however, does not disqualify the suffix pronouns of the latter portions of the inscription from referring to Katimala. The statement that "What I did was to act as servant of Amun, for I did not remember the event which happened to me this year" stands in contrast the obsession with the event apparent in the opening segment of the inscription. This contrast alone appears sufficient to indicate a change in speaker.

The answers remain unclear, but the forcefulness of Katimala's assertion that she in fact succeeded may find some clarification in the light of later Napatan references to military activity. The Napatan rulers did not always lead from the front,[153] and Katimala—whose statement that she accomplished something in the mountains of gold suggests that she was herself present in those mountains—may well be anxious to demonstrate the divine favor that resulted from her personal exertions. In some ways Katimala foreshadows the text of Silko, added to the façade of the temple of Kalabsha,[154] the final direct expression of ancient Nubian military power, and like Katimala's inscription added to the front of an earlier temple. Silko states that he does not follow other rulers, but rather leads (ll. 11–12), and describes his power as manifest both on the plain and in the mountainous regions (l. 15), the old *tꜣ* and *ḫꜣs.t*.

---

[153] Compare the enthronement text of Irike-Ammanote, ll. 26–27 (Macadam, *Kawa* 1, pls. 18 and 23), in which the inscription reports the dispatching of an army, with the statement that the king remained in the palace and did not personally accompany the expedition. Note that later, after receiving a formal conferring of kingship from Amun at Gebel Barkal (ll. 35–43), the king expressly appears to the enemy (l. 46), so perhaps the ruler's remaining in his palace was based more on a ritual than military consideration. Such is not the case in ll. 16–18 of the enthronement text of Anlamani (Macadam, *Kawa* 1, pls. 15–16), however (see also the comments of Sargent, *Napatan Royal Inscriptions*, p. 156, n. 225; for the dispatching of the army compare Spalinger, *Aspects of the Military Documents*, pp. 61–63).

[154] See Bernand, *La prose sur pierre*, vol. 1, pp. 147–49 (No. 67), and vol. 2, pp. 171–73.

Part 3: The Queen Addresses a Council of Chiefs—Fear is the Enemy

Transliteration:

ḫr ḏd=ỉ [5]<*n*> *30 n wr.w*[a] *n*(?) […]

bỉn[b] *pꜣ Pr-ꜥꜣ ḳḳ*[c] *m ḫpš=f*

ỉs.tw[d] *nfr snḏ ỉrm ḫꜣꜥ pḥ.wy*[e] *r-ḥꜣ.t ḫrwy*
mỉ ḳd pꜣ wn nꜣy(=ỉ) ⸢*ỉt.w*⸣ [5-6]*ỉšsp(=ỉ)* [6]*n=w* <*ḥr*> *ỉr(.t)=f*[f]

ḫr ỉỉr … tꜣ rnp.t ḥr tꜣ md.t ỉḫpr ỉr=ỉ[g]

ḫr ỉr nꜣy(=i) ỉt.w ỉwn ssnḏ nꜣ ḫrwy.w nb(.w)[h]
wn=w ḥms
ỉw=w nfr ỉ[rm[i] *nꜣy]=w ḥm.wt*[j]

Translation:

And I said [5]<to> 30 of the chiefs of(?)…

'Bad is the pharaoh who is stripped of his strength.

Is it good to fear, and to show the back before the enemy,
as did (my) ⸢fathers⸣ [6]to whom [5-6](I) succeeded?

[6]Since it was because of the event that occurred to me that … did … in that year.

Now as for (my) fathers who were wont to frighten all the enemies,
they dwelled
happily with their wives.

Text Notes:

[a] The reference to thirty chiefs suggests the old council of the thirty—the *mꜥbꜣy.w* of the *mꜥbꜣy.t*[155]—and reads as though it were a translation of that term, as Grapow, *ZÄS* 76 (1940): 34, suggested. The orthography of *wr.w* as *wry* recalls the word *wrwy* in Caminos, *Tale of Woe,* pls. 5 and 6, col. 2, l. 2.[156]

[b] Ramesses II employs *bin* to describe the defeated rulers of Moab, when he describes the reason for their discomfiture as a result of their alliance with the "other bad man," the ruler of Hatti.[157] *Bin* here recalls the *bin* of l. 2, the evil that befalls those who trust not in Amun.

[155] *Wb.* II 46, 16; Gardiner, *The Admonitions of an Egyptian Sage,* p. 50; Jasnow, in Westbrook, ed., *History of Ancient Near Eastern Law,* p. 265 (§2.1.4.1).

[156] See also Caminos, *Tale of Woe,* p. 90, where Caminos suggests "*wr*, elder; plural *wrwy* (or read *iꜣwy*?);" the example in the inscription of Katimala supports Camino's initial reading *wrwy*.

[157] See Darnell and Jasnow, *JNES* 52 (1993): 263–74.

[c] This verb describing the undesirable condition of a pharaoh is *ḳḳ*, Coptic ⲔⲰⲔ, "to strip,"[158] a word in no wise well attested in the Egyptian lexicon prior to Coptic; Katimala's inscription appears to preserve the earliest written appearance of this word in Egyptian. This passage of the great inscription evokes the question Kamose poses to his advisors at the beginning of his account of the Theban attack against the Hyksos realm:

siꜣ=i sw r iḫ pꜣy=i nḫt
wr m Ḥw.t-wꜥr.t *ky m Kš*
ḥms.kw smꜣ.kw m ꜥꜣm nḥsy

Why do I perceive my power,
with a chief in Avaris, another in Kush,
I finding myself associated with an Asiatic and a Nubian.[159]

[d] The sentence introduced by *ỉst* does not simply express amazement on the part of the speaker.[160] One may suggest that *ỉst* here "denotes concomitance of two events and typically marks a change in the actor or scene";[161] the passage would then contrast what is *bin* with what is apparently *nfr*, but the latter section appears to be somewhat sarcastic in its intent.[162] Essentially, Katimala appears to say that if a ruler stripped of his power is indeed bad—apparently a statement with which all will agree—then terror and retreat are correspondingly good? More simply, this appears to be an example of *ỉst* as a particle introducing a rhetorical question.[163]

[e] On the basis of the determinative, *pḥ.wy* here could be a deverbal noun from *pḥ*, "to reach, etc.," functioning as the object of the verb *ḫꜣꜥ*; one might further suggest a meaning "to desist from attacking."[164] More likely *pḥ.wy* here is the word for "back-

[158] *Wb.* V 71, 12; Crum, *Coptic Dictionary,* pp. 100–101; Westendorf, *KHwb,* p. 59; Černý, *Coptic Etymological Dictionary,* p. 53; Vycichl, *Dictionnaire étymologique,* p. 74. See also Wilson, *Ptolemaic Lexikon,* p. 1070. Only the noun *ḳḳ.t*, "bark," evinces the presence of the word in demotic—see Erichsen, *Demotisches Glossar,* p. 551.

[159] Helck, *Historisch-biographische Texte der 2. Zwischenzeit und neue Texte der 18. Dynastie,* p. 83; Carnarvon and Carter, *Five Years' Explorations,* pl. 28; Habachi, *Second Stela of Kamose,* pl. 5, right, l. 3 below lunette (partially preserved). For the auxiliary use of *ḥmsi* in this passage see Kruchten, *Études de syntaxe néo-égyptienne,* p. 61. For the accumulation of statives see Borghouts, *Lingua Aegyptia* 9 (2001): 11–35, although he appears to ignore the use of certain statives within the groups as auxiliaries.

[160] Černý and Groll, *Late Egyptian Grammar,* p. 556, §61.5.2.

[161] See the discussion of *ỉst* in Manassa, *Great Karnak Inscription of Merneptah,* pp. 136–38.

[162] Compare P. Turin 1882 recto 4, l. 4 (Rossi and Pleyte, *Papyrus de Turin,* pl. 73, II, l. 4): *is.tw nfr pꜣ ir=w n-ḥr=k*, "since what they have done before you is good."

[163] For rhetorical questions see Černý and Groll, *Late Egyptian Grammar,* §61.5; Sweeney, *Correspondence and Dialogue,* p. 106 (and pp. 141–47 on rhetorical questions in letters in general); see also *idem, Lingua Aegyptia* 4 (1994): 287. For the interrogative *ỉst* see also Cassonnet, *Les temps seconds,* pp. 47–49.

[164] For the verb *ḫꜣꜥ* meaning "to abandon," see also Grimal, *Les termes de la propagande,* pp. 603–7.

side," written with the walking legs as an attested variant (*Wb.* I 535), The words *ḫꜣꜥ* and *pḥ.wy* together suggest the Coptic ⲕⲱ ⲉⲡⲁϩⲟⲩ / ⲕⲟⲩ ⲁⲡⲁϩⲟⲩ,[165] "leave behind, set aside," although there no preposition *r* preceding *pḥ.wy*, whereas *r* of *r-ḫꜣ.t* is written. More probably the group simply represents *ḫꜣꜥ pḥ.wy*, functioning as a parallel to *ḫꜣꜥ ḥꜣ* (*r*), "to turn the back (to)."[166] In his laud of Sesostris I, Sinuhe contrasts the attacking ruler with the retreating enemy; for those familiar with the New Kingdom image of the ever-aggressive ruler, Katimala's description of her retreating ancestors would have been an image of a true world turned upside down.[167]

[f] For the relative of *wn* converting a first present, see Junge, *Late Egyptian Grammar,* p. 161.

[g] The inscription clearly writes the status pronominals of *r*, supporting the reading *iḫpr rr=n* in l. 2 (see above).

[h] For *ḫr ir* + noun see Neveu, *La particule ḫr en néo-égyptien,* pp. 97–101. The form *i.wn ssnḏ* is a good late Late Egyptian construction and orthography, and the presence of the prothetic *yodh* in *i.wn* with following infinitive suggests the generality of such a form in Third Intermediate Period texts.[168] The durative sense of the preterite *wn=w ḥms*[169] well suits the passage. One might also render *nꜣ ḫrwy.w nb* (*.w*) as "those (already mentioned) enemies," following Gunn's suggestion that at least in some instances *nꜣ* with plural strokes is "more definitely demonstrative, often corresponding to English 'those.'"[170]

[i] The tops of the two slanting strokes of *irm* (here more or less vertical in orientation) survive above the damage, the orthography of *irm* thus corresponding to that of *irm* in col. 5.

---

[165] Crum, *Coptic Dictionary,* p. 97b; Westendorf, *KHwb,* p. 56.

[166] *Wb.* III, 227, 18; Meeks, *Année lexicographique* 2 (1978), p. 271, no. 78.2931. The best parallel to *ḫꜣꜥ pḥ.wy* in Katimala's inscription appears in P. Brooklyn 47.218.135 col. 5/18—see Jasnow, *Late Period Wisdom Text,* pp. 110–11, who suggests: "As *pḥ.wy* denotes the lower part of the back, the gesture may be rather cruder than that of merely turning one's back."

[167] See Sinuhe §§30–31 (Koch, *Sinuhe,* p. 34):

pḏ nmt.wt pw sk=f bhꜣ.w	wide striding when he destroys the fugitives
nn pḥwy n dd n=f sꜣ	(there is no end to the one who shows him the back);
ꜥḥꜥ-ib pw m ꜣ.t sꜣsꜣ	steadfast in the moment of assault;
ꜥnw pw n rdi.n=f sꜣ=f	one who turns the tide, unable to show his back.

Sinuhe employs *ꜥnw* apparently not simply to mean "who turns himself around," which would imply that at least at some point Sesostris would have turned his back; he rather makes use of *ꜥn* in the sense of turning the tide, as Tjehemau employs the term in his rock inscriptions (see Darnell, *ZÄS* 130 [2003]: pl. 7, ll. 15–16).

[168] For the orthography of *i.wn* here compare Peet, *Tomb Robberies* 30, 7, 15 and 30, 8, 3. For the presence of *i.wn* see Winand, *Études de néo-égyptien* 1, pp. 357–58.

[169] See Wente, *JNES* 21 (1962): 307; compare also Layton, *Coptic Grammar,* p. 349.

[170] See Gardiner, *RdÉ* 6 (1951): 119 n. *f* (reference courtesy of H.-W. Fischer-Elfert).

[j] The queen may here allude to her situation, apparently the somewhat unexpected case of a queen who does what her king could not. The verb *ḥmsi* may alone have the sense of contented life (compare the Instruction of Amenemhat I, §Xid). The passage may also relate to the dedicatory inscription of Thutmosis III in the southern portion of the east exterior wall of the temple at Semna, and specifically Katimala may have found inspiration in col. 5: *iw nsw.t Ḫꜥ-kꜣ.w-Rꜥ m tꜣ ḥr ꜥnḫ.w iw ꜥnḫ=f* ⸢*m*⸣ [*nḏm*]-*ib mi Rꜥ-Ḥr-ꜣḫ.ty*, "While King Khaꜥkaurēꜥ was upon earth with the living, he lived in [contentment(?) of] heart even as Rēꜥ-Ḥarakhti …."[171]

Katimala addresses thirty chiefs, a situation that suggests—if the thirty are indeed the successors of the old *mꜥbꜣy.t*—a group of "government officials in their judicial function"[172]—a legal consideration. The thrust of Katimala's address appears to be the condemnation of the previous, male ruler's conduct, and the depiction of her own, successful actions as those that would earlier have blessed the domestic tranquility of her predecessors. The passage of Katimala's inscription here under discussion, Part 3, recalls the text of the Semna Stela of Sesostris III; more specifically it represents the antithesis of the descriptions of the actions of the properly belligerent and militarily aggressive ruler in ll. 8–10 of the main inscription:[173]

wšb md.t mi ḫpr.t im=s
  ḏr-ntt ir gr m-ḫt pḥ
ssḫm-ib pw n ḫrwy

ḳn.t pw ꜣd
ḥs.t pw ḥm-ḫt
ḫm pw mꜣꜥ ꜣr ḥr tꜣš=f
  ḏr-ntt sḏm nḥs(y) r ḫr n rꜣ
in wšb=f dd ḥm=f

ꜣd=t(w) r=f dd=f sꜣ=f
ḥm-ḫt wꜣ=f r ꜣd

Who responds to a matter according to what happened therein;
  for as for silence after attack—
it is strengthening the heart of the enemy.

Aggression is bravery;
retreat is wretchedness.

[171] For the dedicatory inscription see Caminos, *Semna-Kumma* I, pls. 23 and 25 (and note the commentary p. 45); translation of Caminos, *ibid.*, p. 43.

[172] Jasnow, in Westbrook, ed., *Ancient Near Eastern Law,* p. 265 (§2.1.4.1).

[173] See the convenient re-publication of the copy from Budge's *The Egyptian Sudan* in Parkinson, *Voices from Ancient Egypt,* p. 44; Sethe, *Ägyptische Lesestücke,* p. 84, ll. 1–5. For the possible literary influences on the Semna Stela, particularly the Instruction for Merikare and the Hymns to Sesostris III for the section in the quotation above, see Eyre, in Israelit-Groll, ed., *Studies in Egyptology,* pp. 134–65.

The one expelled from his border is a true deserter,
for the Nubian has merely to hear to fall through a word—
answering him is what makes him retreat.

As soon as one is aggressive to him he shows his back—
retreat and he resumes aggression.

Considering that the Semna Stela was erected at the same fortress at which Katimala later left her tableau, one may with reasonable certainty suggest that Katimala probably knew the text of Sesostris' boundary inscription.[174]

The peaceful dwelling of the earlier rulers with their wives is in contrast to the life of the enemies of Egypt, whose ruling families destroy themselves.[175] The women of the enemies of Egypt at times appear more wise and cognizant of the superiority of Egypt than the men of their groups.[176] Katimala apparently strengthens her position by alluding to an interregnum, an inverted world, in which the rightful ruler, presumably her husband, entered in some way into the state more normally reserved for the enemies of Egypt. The wording of the text also recalls the term *iry-ḥms-nfr*, the "good spouse," an epithet that appears to imply sexual partnership.[177] By indicating that the proper, earlier rulers enjoyed a full conjugal relationship, Katimala may suggest that she was not physically close to her own husband, perhaps an oblique way to explain her own assumption of military and apparently royal authority. Katimala addresses her remarks, and perhaps her entire tableau, to the *mʿbꜣy.t*, a judicial conclave of government officials—perhaps she intended them to confirm her in office. Katimala's tableau may be an appeal to legitimize the assumption of royal office she represents as thrust upon her by the failures of her predecessors and the exigencies of her time.

[174] For the original location of the Semna Stela, see Seidlmayer, *SAK* 28 (2000): 233–42. On p. 242 he notes that the texts of Thutmosis III at Semna do not appear to allude to the Stela of Sesostris III. Katimala, however, may well have done so.

[175] See von der Way, *Göttergericht und "heiliger" Krieg,* pp. 59–62; Manassa, *Great Karnak Inscription,* p. 51 n. g.

[176] Compare Darnell, in Mendel and Claudi, eds., *Ägypten im afro-orientalischen Kontext,* pp. 88–89, n. 71.

[177] Clère, *RdÉ* 20 (1968): 171–76; for an early example of the term see Smith, *The Fortress of Buhen,* pp. 101–2. For Arensnuphis in Meroitic religion see Hofmann, in Haase and Temporini, eds., *Aufstieg und Niedergang* II 18.5, pp. 2838–39.

**Part 4: The Queen Addresses a Council of Chiefs—
What is Good and What is Bad**

TRANSLITERATION:

[7]nfr ỉry bỉn m-dỉ pꜣ ⸢nty⸣ bw ỉr=f ꜥm ỉm=f
bỉn ỉry bỉn m-dỉ rḫy(.t) ỉw=f ꜥm

ỉw=f r dỉ.t pꜣ nty ꜥnḫ[a]
ptr n=n ⸢my⸣ [sḏm=n(?)] [n]ꜣy bỉn[b]
[8]ỉw=w ꜥnḫ

bỉn ỉry nfr[c]
ꜥḏꜣ pꜣ ḏd ⸢nṯr⸣[d]

ỉrw iỉr ꜥnḫ[e]
ỉry nfr

TRANSLATION:

[7]It is good to do evil to this one whom he does not know;
it is bad to do evil to people whom he knows.

He shall appoint the one who is alive.
See here—[we have heard(?)] ⸢these⸣ evil ones,
[8]while they were yet alive—

"It is bad to do good.
That which ⸢god⸣ said is false."

Do what makes life—
Do good.

TEXT NOTES:

[a] The reference to appointing the one who is alive recalls, albeit somewhat vaguely and in a syncopated way, a portion of the Enthronement Stela of Aspelta, l.9:[178]

rdi{t}.n=f sw n sꜣ=f mr=f
ḥr nty twt pw n Rꜥ
nsw.t imy ꜥnḫ.w

That he has given it (the crown) to his son, whom he loves,
Is because he is the image of Re,
king amongst the living.

[178] See Sargent, *Napatan Royal Inscriptions,* pp. 175–76.

"The one who is alive," perhaps better "the survivor,"[179] as a reference to the one appointed is probably a reference not only to Katimala as apparent survivor of a disabled and perhaps ultimately deceased ruler, but also to the proper ruler as the one who is gifted by the gods with life (*cf. Wb.* I 198, 3–9). Fischer-Elfert has also suggested (personal communication) that *ꜥnḫ* may sometimes mean "to be active," in which case the passage in question would indicate that the deity favors the properly active ruler, and the section would conclude with an admonition to be active.

[b] The signs following *ptr* in l. 7 could be another writing of the first person plural suffix pronoun *n* with double water signs (compare the two orthographies in l. 2), an element in a *sḏm=f* conjugation of the verb *ptr*. The surviving portions of signs at the beginning of the lacuna—composite *m*-owl with overlapping human arm—suit a writing of the particle *my*, however, attested as an intensifier following the particle *ptr*,[180] supporting a reading of the signs immediately following *ptr* as the preposition *n* plus the first person plural suffix pronoun *n*.[181] Considering that what appears to be the quotation of a group of evil people follows *iw=w ꜥnḫ* at the top of l. 8, one may suggest restoring *sḏm=n* within the lacuna near the bottom of column 7. A conceivable restoration would also be *ptr n=n* [*nꜣ md.wt n*] [*n*]*ꜣy bin*, "Behold [the words of] ⸢these⸣ evil ones."[182]

[c] One might suggest reading *bin iry nfr* <*n*> *ꜥḏꜣ*, but this would not yield the best sense. Most probably this is a statement such as that in P. BM 10052 col. 14, l. 7: *ꜥḏꜣ pꜣ ḏd=f nb*, "All that he said is false."[183] If this is indeed part of a reported statement of the evildoers, then the wicked hereby render a legal verdict[184] regarding the preceding statement, apparently a divine pronouncement. Interestingly, this reads as though it were a negative response by some group of wrongdoers to the question Tanutamun asks of the embassy of northern princes near the end of his "Dream Stela" (ll. 32–33):[185]

> *is mꜣꜥ pw pꜣ ḏꜣis.n=f* *mdt* ⸢*nṯr*⸣ *ḥr=i*
>
> Is that which he contends true?—God has interceded on my behalf

---

[179] For *ꜥnḫ* in the sense of "continue to live, survive," compare Sauneron, *Un traité d'ophiologie,* references in the glossary p. 232.

[180] See Černý and Groll, *Late Egyptian Grammar,* p. 148 (§9.6.1; see also the ex. 799 [p. 293] cited there); see also Erman, *Neuägyptische Grammatik,* p. 170, §361.

[181] For the "ethical dative" following *ptr* see Erman, *Neuägyptische Grammatik,* p. 170 (§360), and pp. 172–73 (§365).

[182] For the seeming contradiction of calling visual attention to a verbal pronouncement, compare the remarks *ibid.,* p. 172 (§364); one should keep in mind, however, that the apparent oddity of seeing words may simply refer to reading the transcript of a statement.

[183] Cited in Groll, *Non-Verbal Sentence Patterns,* p. 42.

[184] For *ꜥḏꜣ* in legal verdicts, as "wrong" as opposed to *mꜣꜥ.t*, "right," see McDowell, *Jurisdiction,* pp. 23–25; note also Winand, *Karnak* 11 (2003): 649 n. *b* to ll. 13–15.

[185] Grimal, *Quatre stèles napatéennes,* p. 16, l. 9, and pls. 4 and 4a.

[d] The traces below the break suit the bottom of a narrow and vertical sign followed by a seated figure, most likely an orthography of *nṯr*. These signs appear to occupy only the right half of their allotted quadrant, suggesting that another sign or small group of signs has intruded from the quadrant above, extending into the left portion of the next quadrant (for signs shifting to the left of succeeding signs, compare *nꜣ* in ll. 1 and 6, *ḥꜣn* of l. 3, *iwn* in l. 6, and *bin* in ll. 7 and 8). Following *ḏd* one may restore a rope coil alone, or perhaps an unusually small version of the coiled rope with plural strokes, as appears in l. 2.

[e] The apparent repetition of *irw/iry* in this passage suggests that the queen may employ an interjection, *iry/irw* as "yes."[186] The queen's command, echoing in a positive way the statement of the evil ones, fits the context of *do ut des* pronouncements on private monuments of the Late Period.[187] Also conceivable would be a reading *ir r ir ꜥnḫ*, "act in order to live."[188] Note also that *iri ꜥnḫ* can mean "to make provision, to provide for someone" (Faulkner, *Concise Dictionary,* p. 44), a meaning also possible in this context.

This portion of Katimala's inscription, with its rather simple emphasis on doing bad to those whom the deity does not know and evil to those whom he knows is somewhat reminiscent of a section of the Bocchoris text—(col. 3, l. 2)[189]—evil directed at God will lead to *bin*-evil; *mnḫ*-beneficence will lead to the same. The moralizing tone of the queen's inscription foreshadows a portion of the Year 6 inscriptions of Taharqa, Cairo Nos. 38269 (from Matana), ll. 8–9, and 48440 (from Coptos), l. 8, in which a passage evoking didactic literature describes the exaltation of *maat* and the denegration of *isf.t*.[190]

---

186 See Edwards, *Oracular Amuletic Decrees,* pp. 2–3 (n. to L 1 recto 20); for repetition compare the possibly similar *ir nfr ir nfr* formula, for which see Marciniak, *Études et travaux* 2 (1968): 25–31; see also *idem, Les inscriptions hiératiques,* pp. 20–36.

187 See Perdu, *RdÉ* 51 (2000): 175–93, particularly pp. 185–89; Jansen-Winkeln, *Sentenzen,* pp. 54–61.

188 Compare statements such as those in Jansen-Winkeln, *Sentenzen,* pp. 54–61 and 68–70.

189 Zauzich, in *Festschrift Papyrus Erzhog Rainer,* pl. 2; for the text see now Thissen, in Blasius and Schipper, eds., *Apokalyptik und Ägypten,* pp. 113–38.

190 Vikentiev, *La Haute crue du Nil,* pp. 28–29, pls. 4 and 6.

Part 5: The Queen Addresses a Council of Chiefs—Make Unto Amun New Lands

TRANSLITERATION:

ỉs.tw nfr ỉr[a] *n ỉmn kꜣyw*[b] *tꜣ(.w)*
ỉw bn tꜣy=f s.t ỉwnꜣ[c]

ḫr ỉr pꜣ nty <ḥr> ỉr <n> ỉmn ktỉ s.t
ḫr ⸢ptr⸣ … šꜣꜥ [9]*pꜣ hrw*
ỉw ns-sw hy [n]ꜣy=ỉ ỉt.w[d]

TRANSLATION:

Is it not good to do/make other lands for Amun,
where there is not his place at all?

For as for the one who makes <for> Amun another place—
Look, he will … down to today,
it belonging to the annals of my fathers.

TEXT NOTES:

[a] The queen may refer to making a land, meaning creating one, or she may continue to refer to martial undertakings, *ỉr tꜣ* referring to "doing" a land, with a connotation of chastisement.[191] With the use of the preposition *n*, the queen perhaps more likely refers to "assigning to, making over to" Amun new lands,[192] essentially annexing them to Amun's cult by incorporating them into the queen's hegemony.

[b] For the unetymological, medial-*ꜣ* of the plural *kꜣwy*, see Jansen-Winkeln, *Spätmittelägyptische Grammatik*, pp. 32–33 (§47), p. 96 (§150).

[c] For *ỉw bn tꜣy=f s.t ỉwnꜣ*, see Vernus, *RdÉ* 36 (1985): 157; Groll, *Non-Verbal Sentence Patterns*, p. 95 no. 280 (citing the similar *iw bn s.t sw.t iwnꜣ* of P. Salt 124 recto 1, 4).[193] Note also Winand, *Lingua Aegyptia* 5 (1997): 223–236 (particularly p. 225 with n. 14, citing the example from the inscription of Katimala, and translating "alors que ce n'est pas du tout sa place").

---

[191] For *ỉr* in the sense "to travel," or "to visit," followed by the direct object describing the area traversed or visited, see *Wb.* I 111, 12; Gardiner, *Notes on the Story of Sinuhe*, p. 97. Note that the *ỉr* in Sinuhe B 257 is not, as Gardiner took it, an example of *ỉr* "to travel," but is an element of the sentence *ỉr.n wꜥr.t hd ỉm=k*, "flight has taken its toll of you"—so Lichtheim, *Ancient Egyptian Literature* 1, p. 231; an inscription in the tomb of the horologist Amenemhat, wherein it is said of Mitanni that Thutmosis I "did" the country "in recompense for crimes" (Helck, *Historisch-biographische Texte der 2. Zwischenzeit und neue Texte der 18. Dynastie*, p. 110, l. 13: *ỉr.n=f s(y) m db3 tmsw(=s?)*, "as recompense for (its ?) evil did he do it ..."; Brunner, *MIO* 4 [1956]: 324, translates literally "er machte sie als Vergeltung für das Böse," without comment on the use of *ỉr* there; see also Simpson, *Heka-Nefer*, p. 50; Assmann, *RdÉ* 30 [1978]: 26 cols. 7–8 for *ỉrỉ mtn*).

[192] See van den Boorn, *Duties of the Vizier*, pp. 259–60.

[193] See Černý, *JEA* 15 (1929): pl. 42.

[d] The term *hy* is an orthography of the earlier *hrwy.t*, the "day-book."[194] Katimala's reference to the *hy* [*n*]*ꜣy=ỉ ỉt.w*, "the annals of my fathers," recalls the reference to the *ꜥr*(*.t*) *hꜣw nꜣy=f it.w*, "the roll of the annals of his fathers" in the Story of Wenamun.[195]

In this portion of her address to the thirty chiefs, the queen appears to claim to incorporate new land into the realm of Amun, not to restore lost territory.[196] This claim to extending the territory of her state suggests that the problems with which she is faced may not all originate simply through loss of territories once under Egypto-Nubian authority. While one must allow that the queen might overlook the formal viceregal control over an area in her subjugation of new and dangerous threats in that area in order to strengthen her position in the eyes of the thirty chiefs, the queen's statement could be a true assessment. If in fact the earlier Medjay dominance of the Eastern Desert and the increasingly Egyptianized Libyan groups of the Western Desert—the dominant forces to the east and west of the Nubian Nile during the New Kingdom—indeed gave way to new nomadic groups,[197] the threat the queen faced may in fact have involved an extension of direct "Nilotic" authority more deeply into the Nubian hinterland (see also p. 60, below). With the ultimate border of direct Egyptian control in New Kingdom Nubia in the region of Kurgus,[198] one may reasonably suggest that the queen may allude to the extension of a proto-Napatan state across the Bayuda Desert, and the incorporation of Meroe into the nascent polity.

Part 6: The Queen Addresses a Council of Chiefs—the Cattle of Amun

TRANSLITERATION:

ỉs.tw bỉn ẖrp[a] *tꜣy ẖrpw*[b] *n ỉmn m mn.t*
nfr šꜥ.t n tꜣ ẖrpw[c] *n ỉmn mỉ ḳd pꜣ* [*iir*] [9–10]*Mkꜣrš*[d]
[10]*ỉw ỉỉr nꜣ n rmṯ*[e] *nb n nỉw.t sḥwr*[f] *Mkꜣršꜣ m mn.t*
ỉw dmy[g] *n=f mỉ ḳd ꜥḏn*
ỉw bw-pwy … =f

[10–11]*bỉn* [11]*pḥww r-ḥꜣ.t=f*[h]
mỉ-ḳd pꜣ [*n*]*ty* <*ḥr*> *pḥw r-ḥꜣ.t pꜣ mšꜥ pꜣ ỉr nfr n tꜣ ḏr=f*
bỉn ỉr n=f pꜣ nty … …

---

[194] See Redford, *Pharaonic King-Lists*, pp. 97–126.

[195] Gardiner, *Late-Egyptian Stories*, p. 68, ll. 1–2.

[196] As does Irike-Ammanote in ll. 60–63 and 65–69 of his enthronement inscription (Macadam, *Kawa* 1, pls. 19 and 24).

[197] Compare Sadr, *Nomadism*, pp. 112–13.

[198] J. Vercoutter, *Kush* 4 (1956): 70; Davies, *Sudan and Nubia* 2 (1998): 29–30; Welsby and Davies, eds., *Uncovering Ancient Sudan*, pp. 40–41; Davies, *Sudan and Nubia* 5 (2001): 46–58; *idem*, *Sudan and Nubia* 7 (2003): 52–54; *idem*, *BSFE* 157 (2003): 23–37.

TRANSLATION:

Is it bad to control this cattle of Amun daily?
Is it good to sacrifice from the herd of Amun, like that [which] Makaresh [did]?
[10]since daily all the city people cursed Makaresh,
while there afflicted him likewise destruction,
[...] not having done(?) [...]

[10-11]Is it evil [11]to flee before him,
like the one who flees before the army of the one who does good for the entire land?
Evil is doing for him that which ...

TEXT NOTES:

[a] The verb *ḫrp* here, referring to cattle could—under the influence of uses such as *Wb.* III 327, 10—have the specific meaning "to drive to offering, to sacrifice." The rhetorical question suggests that it is in fact good to *ḫrp* this cattle of Amun, and the specific meaning of the verb *ḫrp* is probably that of *Wb.* III 327, 1, "Rinder antreiben;"[199] here the verb appears to describe the benevolent direction of Katimala's rule.[200] In her reference to her *ḫrp*-control the queen apparently has no fear of evoking, albeit somewhat distantly, a portion of the Prophecy of Neferti: *ʿnd tꜣ ʿšꜣ ḫrp.w=f*, "As the land decreases so the directors increase."[201]

[b] The term *ḫrpw* for cattle (*Wb.* III 329, 15), apparently "sacrificial cattle," appears in an inscription of Taharqa from Karnak.[202] In Katimala's inscription the term appears as a feminine collective.

[c] In *nfr šʿ.t n tꜣ ḫrpw* we have *m* > *n* before the dental of *tꜣ*. The opening lines of Part 6 echo chiastically those of Part 4, the references to *bin* and *nfr* of Part 4 becoming *nfr* and *bin* of Part 6:

Part 6	Part 4
i͗s.tw bi͗n ḫrp tꜣy ḫrpw ...	*nfr i͗ry bi͗n m-di͗ pꜣ nty ...*
nfr šʿ.t n tꜣ ḫrpw ...	*bi͗n i͗ry bi͗n m-di͗ rḫy(.t) ...*

The chiasm also involves an increasing emphasis on *bin*-evil. Also possible would be a nominal *sḏm=f* of *šʿ*, *šʿ=tw* as the subject of *nfr*.

---

199 The *Belegstellen*'s one citation is to an appropriate scene of men driving plowing cattle—see Tylor and Griffith, *Paheri,* pl. 3, third register of field scenes from the top, text before leftmost driving plowman.

200 Compare Wilson, *Ptolemaic Lexikon,* pp. 746–47 (specifically the reference to Edfou I 143, 5 "the king controls the living in the whole land").

201 Helck, *Die Prophezeiung des Nfr.tj,* p. 42, §XIb.

202 Vernus, *BIFAO* 75 (1975): 51 n. h.

d The name appears otherwise unattested.[203] Note, however, the not dissimilar *Mrḳšt*, a feminine name of Eighteenth Dynasty date belonging to a Nubian in P. Berlin 9784, 12.[204]

e The orthography of *rmṯ*, with the second phonetic sign interpreted as *r*,[205] results from a misunderstanding of the proper hieroglyphic representation of the hieratic.

f The description of the city's reaction to the obscure Makaresh is desribed as *sḥwr*, "to curse," a reference that could refer simply to the anger of the city dwellers directed at the unfortunate Makaresh, or to a more elaborate, culticly sanctioned magical procedure.[206]

g The juridical use of *dmi* (*Wb.* V 454, 17) suggests a reference to the actual punishment of Makaresh. The term *ʿḏn* here may be that of *Wb.* V 241, 16, probably identical with Coptic ⲱϫⲛ.[207]

h What appears to be *pḥww* may be an orthography of *pḥrr*, "to run;" for the orthography with the *pḥ*-rump compare the Twentieth Dynasty example in *Wb.* I 541. For the writing note also the alternation of *pḥ* and *pḥrr* in *Wb.* I 541, 10–11. The flesh sign determining *r-ḥꜣ.t* in the first occurrences is augmented by the addition of the heart in the second.

The reference to a sacrifice from the herd of Amun could be a euphemistic reference to murder;[208] according to Admonitions 12, 1 and Loyalist Teaching §13, 8, regarding the improper ruler: *ʿnḏ idr=f*, "his herd will decline." Alternatively, improper use of the cattle attached to a cult appears not infrequently in surviving documents,[209]

---

203 Ranke, *Personennamen* 2, 292, no. 23, lists the name with only this occurrence, designating the name as Nubian and giving it a Twenty-Second Dynasty date.

204 See Ranke, *Personennamen* 1, p. 163, no. 9; Gardiner, *ZÄS* 43 (1906): pl. 1 and p. 29.

205 Compare the "abnormal writings" cited in Faulkner, *Concise Dictionary,* p. 150.

206 On *sḥwr* see Müller-Wollermann, *Vergehen und Strafen,* pp. 157–59.

207 Compare the remarks of Edwards, *Oracular Amuletic Decrees,* p. 66, n. 61; for *ʿḏn*/*ʿḏny.t* see also von Deines and Westendorf, *Wörterbuch der medizinischen Texte, erste Hälfte,* p. 159. For the Coptic see Černý, *CED* p. 233; Westendorf, *KHwb,* p. 298; Vycichl, *Dictionnaire étymologique,* p. 252 (all citing Erichsen, *Demotisches Glossar,* p. 75); the noun "ceasing, destruction," is Crum, *Coptic Dictionary,* p. 539b–540a.

208 For mankind as the cattle of god see *inter alia* Posener, *L'Enseignement loyaliste,* pp. 40, 47, and 48; Parkinson, *Poetry and Culture,* p. 209, and the references cited there; note also l. 5 of the Aspelta Enthronement Stela—Grimal, *Quatre stèles napatéennes,* p. 24 and pls. 6 and 6a. Compare the statement of the commanders of the army in the enthronement text of Irike-Ammanote (Macadam, *Kawa* 1, pls. 17 and 22), ll. 8, in which they compare themselves to *ʿw.t iwtt mniw*, "the herd without herdsman." The "sacrifice" might be less violent, perhaps taking the form of banishment—compare von Beckerath, *RdÉ* 20 (1968): 11, l. 23, with pp. 26–27 and 35, who suggests that so violent a phrase as *smꜣ rmṯ ʿnḫ* (l. 23) may refer to banishment.

209 So P. Turin 1887 recto I, 2–3; II, 14–15 (Gardiner, *Ramesside Administrative Documents,* pp. 74 and 77); recent translation by Vittmann, in Porten, ed., *The Elephantine Papyri,* pp. 45–56; see also Haring, *Divine Households,* pp. 254–56 and 369; Goebs, *JEA* 89 (2003): 27–37; Fischer-Elfert, *Annals of the Naprstek Museum* 24 (2003): 73–87.

such incidents are not unknown to the Napatan royal inscriptions,[210] and reference to a sacred herd of Amun would be well in keeping with the inscription's emphasis on the power of Amun, who may appear himself as a divine steer.[211] The cattle associated with the cult of Amun were numerous at Napata during the Twenty-Fifth Dynasty.[212]

Curiously, even though Makaresh appears to have been accursed, his name receives the determinative of the squatting "revered man" (A52), somewhat unexpected for an "excommunicate" such as Makaresh. Nevertheless, in the Excommunication Stela, the condemned group receives a normal seated man determinative;[213] less surprising perhaps than the sign A52 determining the name of Makaresh, but again not the sign one might expect for an enemy. Katimala's inscription refers to military activity against a group of desert dwellers, or at least some group active in a mountainous region, and follows with a formal address to a group of chiefs, making allusion to some cattle, real or metaphoric; the inscription of Irike-Ammanote (*Kawa* IX) also describes an attack by desert dwellers during the time between the death of Talakhamani and his successor, with the army commanders asking themselves why they are "[wan]dering like small cattle without a herder."[214] Perhaps Katimala's inscription echoes a similar situation.

A certain chiastic parallelism is apparent in the construction of Parts 3–6 of the inscription, the queen's address to the thirty chiefs. Parts 3 and 5 are similar, as are Parts 4 and 6:

Part 3	Part 5
is.tw nfr …	*is.tw nfr …*
mi-ḳd …	*iw bn …*
ḫr iir …	*ḫr ir …*
ḫr ir …	*ḫr ptr …*
wn=w …	*iw ns-sw …*
iw=w …	

Part 4	Part 6
nfr iry …	*is.tw bin ḫrp …*
bin iry …	*nfr šʿ.t …*
bin iry nfr	*bin …*
	bin …

[210] From the Napatan inscription compare the claim by Aspelta in l. 7 of the Khaliut Stela (M.B. Reisner, *ZÄS* 70 [1934]: 40–41) not to have done such, and the reference in ll. 22–24 of the enthronement stela of Irike-Ammanote (Macadam, *Kawa* 1, pls. 17 and 22) to rebels who have come to plunder cattle, people, and the other property thereof.

[211] Compare Bakr, *ZÄS* 98 (1970): 1–4; Kormysheva, in Berger, Clerc, and Grimal, eds., *Hommages à Jean Leclant* 2, pp. 259–60.

[212] Compare ll. 22–24 of the Dream Stela of Tanutamun—Grimal, *Quatre stèles napatéennes,* p. 13, ll. 1–5, and pls. 3 and 3a. Later members of a herd of Amun may appear in Chapman and Dunham, *Decorated Chapels,* pls. 8 and 15.

[213] Grimal, *Quatre stèles napatéennes,* p. 38, ll 5 and 7.

[214] Pierce, in Eide, Hägg, Pierce, and Török, *Fontes Historiae Nubiorum* 2, p. 401.

Part 7: The Fragmentary Conclusion

The remaining, final portion of the text is badly damaged, principally the result of the confluence of block joints in the area. Given the idiosyncratic nature of Katimala's text to this point, restorations of the end of the inscription—though tempting—are at best tenuous. The glossary below includes no entries to words after l. 11, and what follows is but an attempt to represent and interpret those words one might with something approaching confidence read in the damaged text. Similarly, the hieroglyphic transcription of the text represents only those signs for which restorations of the surviving traces seem probable.

The lines of the main inscription, slanting increasingly to the left toward the bottom, as one moves left through the inscription, in the end encroach upon the goddess Isis, and the surviving elements of the final line are much cramped, especially between the goddess' elbow and the *ʿnḫ*-sign she holds in her lowered hand.

TRANSLITERATION:

... *ꜣ*(?) *ptpt* ... *rḫ*.[*k*?]*wỉ*
ỉw=ỉ ỉr w(?) ...
... *r=ỉ mỉ-ḳd*
rn=ỉ(?) *ỉirw*(?) ...
rn=⌜*k*⌝(?) *iir*(?) ...[a]

TRANSLATION:

... trampling ... I know,
while I act ...
... against/toward me, entirely.
It is my reputation (?) that has made(?) ...
It is ⌜your⌝ reputation(?) that has made(?) ...

TEXT NOTE:

[a] Though so sadly damaged, the final portion of l. 13 may contain two references to *rn*, "name" or "character." If this is correct, the text may here echo a portion of an inscription of Thutmosis III on the outer face of the west wall of Semna Temple:[215]

rn(=*i*) *pw ḫnty nṯr.w* *rn=k pw ḫnty ʿnḫ.w*

"As my name is pre-eminent among the gods,
so is your name pre-eminent among the living".

[215] Caminos, *Semna-Kumma* 1, pl. 39, l. 21; the following translation is *ibid.*, p. 77.

Dating the Inscription — Palaeography and Grammar

Palaeographic Considerations

Katimala's inscription does not employ entirely standardized hieroglyphic signs, and this may have contributed to the characterizations of the inscription as "awkward in shape and of ungainly appearance."[216] Fortunately for dating purposes, a number of the signs reveal clear hieratic orthographies. The signs in Katimala's main inscription demonstrating sufficient cursive and semi-cursive palaeographic peculiarities to allow for some attempt at dating the script point to an earlier rather than later date for the inscription. Palaeographically the script of Katimala's inscription suggests in general a date prior to the end of the sixth century BCE, and supports more specifically—and with a preponderance of evidence—a date during the Twenty-First Dynasty (although not excluding entirely a date in the Twenty-Second Dynasty).[217] The sign forms in the inscription are, as one might expect, closer to the forms occurring in literary texts than to those of the non-literary tradition.[218] The following notes should elaborate upon the accompanying palaeographic chart (fig. 1).

D28: The *kꜣ*-arms are more in the tradition of Twenty-First and Twenty-Second Dynasty forms, although this alone is not a strong palaeographic argument.[219]

F26: The *ḥn*-sign in l. 1 has more the appearance of a feline quadruped than the expected headless bovine body. The form of the sign as it appears in Katimala's inscription apparently derives from a misinterpretation of hieratic forms such as those in Möller, *Hieratische Paläographie* III, p. 15, no. 165 (Leinwand and P. Bremner examples).[220]

---

[216] Caminos, *Semna-Kumma* 1, p. 24; he also states (*ibid.*): "Apart from their inelegance, the hieroglyphs in the main inscription are quite deficient in clarity and legibility."

[217] Grapow, *ZÄS* 76 (1940): 28, appears to have erred on all counts when he claimed that "Die so stehengebliebenen hieratischen … Zeichen passen etwa in die Perserzeit, können aber auch älter sein; als Alterskriterium sind sie kaum sicher zu beurteilen und zu verwenden."

[218] Compare conveniently the collection in Wimmer, *Hieratische Paläographie der nicht-literarischen Ostraka* 2.

[219] Compare Verhoeven, *Untersuchungen zur späthieratischen Buchschrift*, p. 118.

[220] Compare also Goyon, *Le Papyrus d'Imouthès*, p. 5 (particularly the examples from P. Brooklyn 47.218.50, to be dated to the early to middle sixth century BCE—see Verhoeven, *Untersuchungen zur späthieratischen Buchschrift*, p. 318). Note also a number of the examples in *ibid.* pp. 130–31 (and p. 235: "Am Hals entsteht z.T. ein gegabeltes Ende"). Note also the odd forms that can appear to have head and ears, as in Gasse, *Données nouvelles*, palaeographic pl. 14.

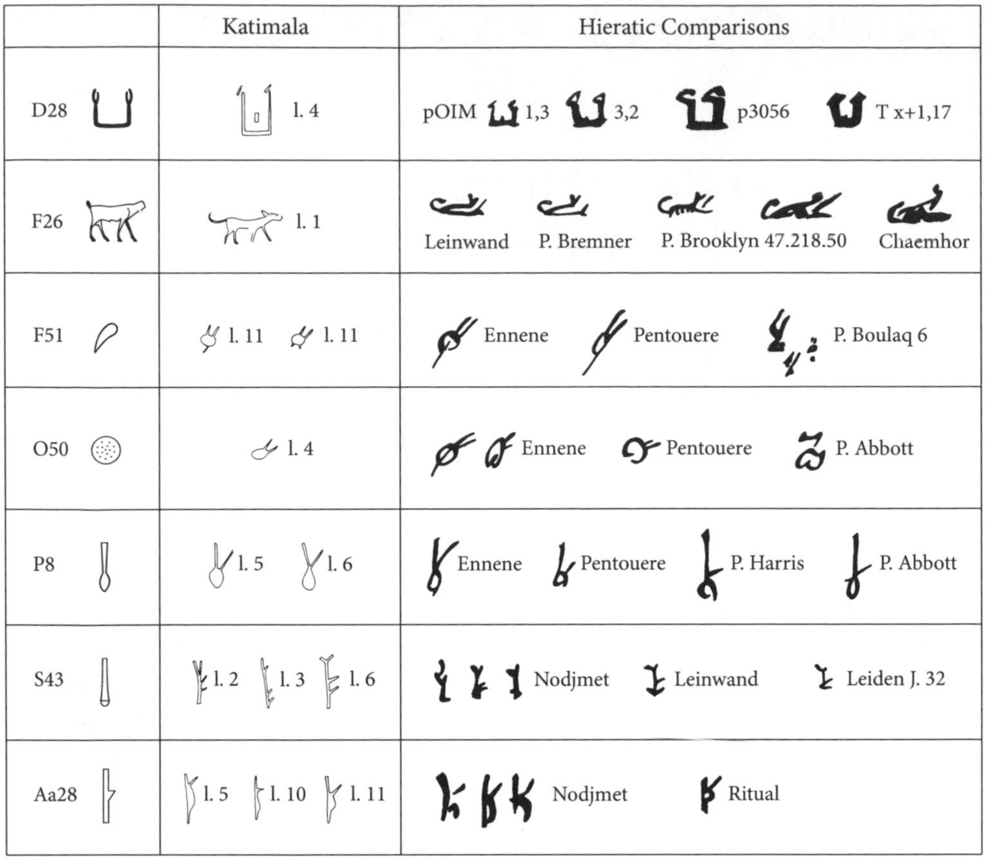
Katimala
Hieratic Comparisons
D28
l. 4
pOIM 1,3 3,2 p3056 T x+1,17
F26
l. 1
Leinwand
P. Bremner
P. Brooklyn 47.218.50
Chaemhor
F51
l. 11 l. 11
Ennene
Pentouere
P. Boulaq 6
O50
l. 4
Ennene
Pentouere
P. Abbott
P8
l. 5 l. 6
Ennene
Pentouere
P. Harris
P. Abbott
S43
l. 2 l. 3 l. 6
Nodjmet
Leinwand
Leiden J. 32
Aa28
l. 5 l. 10 l. 11
Nodjmet
Ritual

FIG. 1 *Hieratic palaeographic chart.*

F51: The flesh sign is similar to the Ennene and Pentouere examples in Möller, *Hieratische Paläographie* II, p. 15, no. 178.[221] Although there are excellent examples of the sign with this appearance in P. Pushkin 127, such a form of F51 with dual protrusions to the top appears neither in late hieratic texts, nor in the abnormal hieratic script, although standard demotic forms of the sign derive from such a shape.[222]

O50: The *sp*-sign has two strokes at the top, as does the flesh sign. This is a feature of the sign in the Ennene, Pentoere, and P. Abbott examples in Möller, *Hieratische Paläographie* II, p. 36, no. 403 (note also the P. Louvre 3230 and Pet. 1116 Ar145 examples in the *Nachträge,* pp. 5 and 9),[223] but absent from the Möller, *Hieratische Paläographie* III, p. 38, no. 403 examples.[224]

[221] Compare also Koenig, *Boulaq 6,* p. 7.

[222] See Caminos, *Tale of Woe,* pl. 3, ll. 12 and 14, etc. Regarding the lack of later versions of F51 with protrusions compare the examples in Verhoeven, *Untersuchungen sur späthieratischen Buchschrift,* pp. 134–35; for the abnormal hieratic and demotic signs see El-Aguizy, *A Palaeographical Study of Demotic Papyri,* pp. 80–81 and 314–15.

[223] Compare also Koenig, *Boulaq 6,* pls. 2a, l. 1, and 3a, l. 6.

[224] Double protrusions at the top are also absent from the forms of F51 collected in Verhoeven, *Untersuchungen zur späthieratischen Buchschrift,* pp. 134–35 (see also p. 243).

P8: The *ḫrw*-sign in Katimala's inscription is more like those of Möller, *Hieratische Paläographie* II, p. 34, no. 381 (Merneptah to Twenty-First Dynasty) than the shapes in Möller, *Hieratische Paläographie* III, p. 36, no. 381.[225]

S43: The *mdw*-stick is uniformly of a modified hieratic shape, with forked top and twin protrusions from the right side. Such a form is similar to Möller, *Hieratische Paläographie* II, p. 40, no. 456 (*Nḏm.t*) and *idem, Hieratische Paläographie* III, p. 43, no. 456 (Leinwand and later examples), closest in appearance to the *Nḏm.t* 8, 2 example.[226] In fact, a number of other close parallels, having protrusions from the right side, but lacking any foot or base to the vertical, appear to cluster around the Twenty-First Dynasty.[227]

Aa28: The *ḳd*-sign finds close parallels in Möller, *Hieratische Paläographie* II, p. 44, no. 488 (*Nḏm.t*) and *idem, Hieratische Paläographie* III, p. 46, no. 488 (Ritual), with the *Nḏm.t* examples providing the closest parallels to the form of Aa28 in Katimala's inscription.

Grammar of the Inscription

The grammar of Katimala's inscription fits well with an apparent date during the early Third Intermediate Period. Grammatically the queen speaks to us in a form of Late Egyptian, tinged with demotic and proto-Coptic elements (the grammatical index following the glossary summarizes the various forms occurring in the inscription). The most pronounced of the latter, the three apparent occurrences of (ⲉ)ⲙⲙⲟⲛ ⲧⲁⲣⲉϥϣⲱⲡⲉ (l. 2), occur in the quotation of the male ruler's "political lament," and are perhaps the result of actual use of a later phase, or one might say more colloquial level, of the language. At the very least the composer of the inscription may have employed such a level of the language in the otherwise "high Late Egyptian" text in order to provide a more colloquial, perhaps even coarser edge to the king's complaint. Late Middle Egyptian intrusions into the queen's account are distinctly lacking, and the language level of the inscription is essentially that in which an educated epistolographer of the Ramesside Period functioned.[228]

---

[225] Note, however, the rare archaizing form in *ibid.*, pp. 42–43, example no. 21.

[226] Note also the forms collected *ibid.*, pp. 184–85, those of her examples most closely resembling the appearance on S43 in Katimala's inscription finding place under the headings "TB Greenfield, pOIM 18039" and "'Takelothis', div. pBerlin."

[227] Compare Koenig, *Boulaq 6*, pl. 5a, l. 7; Edwards, *Oracular Amuletic Decrees*, pl. 17, P. L. 7, 55 (lacking base, but with only a single protrusion to the right side; for the date of the papyrus see also the comments of Jacquet-Gordon, *Bi.Or.* 20 [1963]: 32; compare also the examples in Caminos, *Tale of Woe*, pl. 3, l. 12, pl. 5, l. 4). For versions of the sign with forked top and twin right protrusions, but with base, see the examples in Verhoeven, *Untersuchungen zur späthieratischen Buchschrift*, p. 184.

[228] Amongst the numerous possible references see Jansen-Winkeln, *WZKM* 85 (1995): 92–102; and Goldwasser, in Groll, ed., *Studies in Egyptology Presented to Miriam Lichtheim* 1, pp. 200–240. See also the useful discussion of language levels in a Ramesside monumental text in Manassa, *Great Karnak Inscription of Merneptah*, pp. 151–52.

Conclusion

The inscription of Katimala is composed in what appears to be a form of Late Egyptian tinged with what one might term demotic and early Coptic elements. The style of the carving and the decoration appear to belong to the earlier, Ramesside tradition, so far as one may judge.[229] The signs of the thirteen columns of text that form the main inscripiton are grouped in Ramesside fashion, arranged in word squares composed of essentially nine potential smaller units,[230] albeit somewhat tightly packed and even to an extent jumbled in places.[231] Although employing the hieroglyphic script, the grammar of the inscription is not based on Third Intermediate Period Egyptian hieroglyphic texts, themselves deriving from nonliterary Ramesside Late Middle Egyptian grammar.[232] The purity of the Late Egyptian grammar in Katimala's inscription, compared to the often not unsuccessful striving after Middle Egyptian forms in the stelae of Piye and Tanutamun, and the increasing demotico-Coptic features of the later Napatan historical inscriptions (such as the Stele of Enthronement, the Stela of Harsiotef, and the Stele of Nestasen), might at first suggest that Katimala's inscription belongs with the latter group of later Napatan texts.[233] Hieratic and hieraticizing aspects of the inscription's palaeography, however, firmly support a Twenty-First Dynasty/early Third Intermediate Period date for the inscription.

---

[229] Compare the observations of Morkot, in Wenig, ed., *Studien zum antiken Sudan,* p. 145.

[230] Compare the discussion in Loprieno, *Ancient Egyptian,* pp. 21–22.

[231] Compare Caminos, in Caminos and Fischer, *Epigraphy,* p. 5, n. 6, who comments on the accuracy of Weidenbach's 1844, free-hand copy of the Katimala tableau.

[232] See conveniently Jansen-Winkeln, *Spätmittelägyptische Grammatik* on this.

[233] For the grammar of the Classical Egyptian Napatan texts (the Dream Stela of Tanutamun, the Enthronement Inscription of Anlamani, the Enthronement Stela of Aspelta, the Khaliut Stela, the Stela of Excommunication, the Enthronement Inscription of Irike-Ammanote), and that of the Late Egyptian Napatan texts (the Adoption Stela of Aspelta, the Stelae of Harsiotef and Nestasen), see Sargent, *Napatan Royal Inscriptions*; for the latter group see also Peust, *Das Napatanische.*

Literary Form and a Theory of Kingship

Caminos has noted that Katimala's graceful figure shows none of what he somewhat immoderately terms the "barbaric" obesity of later depictions of Nubian queens, and indeed there is nothing "barbaric" to Katimala's language as it appears in the text of her Semna inscription. The scene and its accompanying annotations are more nicely laid out than the columns of the main inscription, columns that grow increasingly askew and slant down towards the left. Nevertheless, in spite of the irregularity of the columns themselves, the inscription itself is not irregular.

The main inscription of Katimala's Semna tableau is not a "letter to the dead," as has been suggested.[234] Such a view of the text appears to rest not on readings of the inscription but rather on a statement Grapow made near the end of his examination of the inscription: "Aber die Sprache unseres Textes ist allzu nahe verwandt der Sprache des Papyrus Neskhons und ähnlicher Texte, als daß hier nicht auch inhaltliche Verbindung angenommen werden darf."[235] Katimala's inscription is in fact not far removed in either date of composition or grammatical features from the Neskhons text. Katimala's inscription does not, however, have much in common with the Neskhons text when one examines the content of the compositions. Neither grammar nor content provide any indication that Katimala's inscription is a letter to or from the dead,[236] nor is magical practice or mortuary religion of any sort at the heart of the queen's inscription. Her text is a document of royal piety, set within what appears to be a context of native despair and foreign evil.

If the inscription of Katimala is indeed of roughly the time of the Twenty-First Dynasty in Egypt—or perhaps even as late as the Twenty-Second Dynasty—as grammar and palaeography indicate, then the paucity of epigraphic and archaeological evidence from elsewhere in Nubia, and the relatively primitive state of the earliest of

[234] Compare the comments of Kendall, in Wenig, ed., *Studien zum antiken Sudan,* pp. 4 and 60–63. Pierce, in Eide, Hägg, Pierce, and Török, *Fontes Historiae Nubiorum* 1, p. 40, describes the decree of Amun for Neskhons, and then compares that decree to the inscription of Katimala: "Though the affairs are obviously different, the two texts are based on similar interpretations of magic and reflect the same concept of the deceased acting in the sphere of the living as an intermediary or as a dangerous force." Török, *CRIPEL* 17/1 (1995): 212 with n. 58, states that the text "commemorates a queen who was expected to act as intermediary between Amun and a king in a difficult situation," and claims that "textual as well as conceptual features show an affinity with the Nesikhons Papyrus."

[235] Grapow, *ZÄS* 76 (1940): 41.

[236] Third Intermediate Period letters to the dead appear to be composed in Middle Egyptian, with Late Egyptian influences—see Jansen-Winkeln, *Text und Sprache in der 3. Zwischenzeit,* p. 201.

the el-Kurru royal burials, itself apparently of later date than Katimala's Semna tableau, are all features that make Katimala's inscription all the more remarkable for the purity of its Late Egyptian grammar and the complexity of its composition. Writing in a language possibly not their own, Katimala and her scribes composed an innovative inscription, making new use of older literary forms.

The general organization of the text is not without literary merit. The inscription opens with the address of an unnamed male ruler to Katimala. He laments a bad situation in which he and his realm find themselves, thereby providing some—albeit nebulous—background information. Katimala then addresses the reader(?), and describes the final good outcome of the strife. She then refers to the coming of the discomfited male ruler, the one who first spoke. This portion of the inscription returns the reader to the event with which the inscription opened, an event in fact anterior in time to the victories and later address of Katimala. The queen then records a rather lengthy address she made to a council of thirty chiefs. Her address itself constitutes a personal "loyalist teaching" of adherence to the cult of Amun. The address appears to contain some sort of political parable, referring to a crime against the cattle of Amun, perpetrated by a certain Makaresh.

The author of the text was acquainted with a number of earlier literary forms (such as military compositional style, the *Königsnovelle,* and wisdom literature), and probably knew and made conscious allusion to specific earlier, Middle Egyptian texts.[237] The initial pronouncement of the defeated male ruler, whom Katimala almost immediately afterwards says had come to her, is redolent of the initial *iw=tw* formula of earlier, New Kingdom military writings,[238] wherein a messenger brings news of dire events on the border of the pharaonic realm. In essence, the ruler makes report to Katimala of the dire circumstances of enemy activity against the ordered state. The queen then states that she succeeded; rather than providing even a poetically filtered image of battlefield tactics, we glimpse only fleetingly some hint at overall strategy involving the mining regions of the Eastern Desert(?). The queen is in fact most concerned with providing the ideological and religious underpinnings of her victory—the worship of Amun and the proper trust in the power of the deity. She continues in the general outline of New Kingdom military texts with a lengthy "result" section, in which she addresses a council of thirty chiefs, and presumably

[237] These and other references to earlier literature in the later Napatan texts (see for instance the examples gathered by Jasnow, in Teeter and Larson, eds., *Gold of Praise,* pp. 193–210) speak against any view that speakers and writers of later phases of Egyptian lacked proper understanding of Middle Egyptian (as Depuydt, *SAK* 27 [1999]: 38–44, assumed). No more inaccurate assessment of the text can be found than that of Török, *Birth of an Ancient African Kingdom,* p. 49: "The genre of the text is only partly monumental (dating and narrative sections) and gives the impression of a half-educated author and of a commissioner who was not aware of the Egyptian traditions of royal utterances and of the nature of king-deity interaction;" he takes this to be the work of "poorly educated *literati.*" This is similar to the inaccurate assumptions some have made regarding the earlier inscriptions of the Nubian soldier Tjehemau (see the references cited in Darnell, *ZÄS* 130 [2003]: 32–33), and both seem to rest on a biased assumption of scribal uncouthness south of the First Cataract.

[238] See Spalinger, *Aspects of the Military Documents,* pp. 1–33 *et passim.*

received their accolades.[239] The royal address is a feature of the earlier *Königsnovellen*, appearing also in the more sober and Day-Book derived Annals of Thutmosis III, and in the Great Karnak Inscription of Merneptah.[240]

Katimala's text provides evidence of a long-standing Egyptian theory of kingship, in which the rightful ruler is one who properly cares for his or her ancestors, shepherds his or her human flock, and attends to the divine cults.[241] Placing her text on the façade of Semna Temple, Katimala advertises her struggle as one ultimately designed to ensure the hegemony of Amun; her tableau is in essence a spiritual donation text, a Nubian version of Third Intermediate Period Egyptian documents of royal legitimation.[242] No matter that her male predecessor may have failed in his attempts to subdue his enemies, and no matter that the tone of the queen's text may to some extent disparage the conduct of the inept male ruler—primarily through the implication that he lacked sufficient faith in Amun—Katimala nevertheless appears to have avenged the death of that ruler. If the king who became disabled were in fact Katimala's husband, then the queen fulfilled the role of the goddess Isis, and an equation of the queen with Isis through this role of avenger could go far to explaining the prominence of Isis in the pictorial portion of Katimala's tableau.[243]

Katimala's inscription not only fits well into an Egyptian tradition of proper rulership, her tableau at Semna stands—in terms of both date and prominence—at or at least very near the head of a tradition of important female administrators of the Third Intermediate Period. Katimala was a female ruler, who appears to have gone from being *ḥm.t-nsw.t* to fulfilling the role of *nsw.t-bity* in her own right. In her tableau she steps out of the role of feminine supporter of the warrior ruler, and beyond the human incarnation of the protective force of the goddess of the Eye of the Sun,[244] and becomes herself both the righteously militant ruler and the object of the protection of the Eye of the Sun. Katimala's political prominence may find some precursor in an earlier Egyptian execration text of early Twelfth Dynasty date, in which at least one woman appears to have exercised sole rule over a Nubian state.[245] The importance

[239] Compare the remarks *ibid.*, pp. 87–96.

[240] For the *Königsnovelle* see Jansen-Winkeln, *WZKM* 83 (1993): 101–16; Hofmann, *Königsnovelle*; Manassa, *Great Karnak Inscription*, pp. 107–9; for later Napatan relections of the *Königsnovelle* see Breyer, *Tanutamani*, pp. 269–70.

[241] Compare in general, from amongst the numerous possible references, the various chapters in O'Connor and Silverman, eds., *Ancient Egyptian Kingship*; Johnson, *JSSEA* 13 (1983): 61–72 (for the theory of kingship in the Demotic Chronicle see also Felber, in Blasius and Schipper, eds., *Apokalyptik und Ägypten*, pp. 106–10; Hoffmann, *Ägypten*, pp. 177–80).

[242] See Bickel, Gabolde, and Tallet, *BIFAO* 98 (1998): 48–49.

[243] Compare Johnson, *JSSEA* 13 (1983): 68, referring to the Demotic Chronicle 3, 12–14.

[244] Compare the remarks of Roth, *Gebieterin aller Länder*, pp. 23–42.

[245] See ll. 1–3 of Cairo JdE 63957, an execration figure (or as Posener suggests perhaps better called a proscription figure) dating probably from late in the reign of Sesostris I or early in the reign of Amenemhat II: *ḥḳꜣ.t ny.t Iꜣm-nꜥs Sꜥṯyt*(?) *ms.t.n mw.t=s ḏd.t r=s ny smꜣ… mšꜥ=s*, "The female ruler of Iam-nas, Satjyt(?), born of her mother, called 'not …;' her army" (Posener, *Cinq figurines d'envoûtement*, p. 29, pls. 1 and 6).

of Katimala at the dawn of Napatan royal power supports the significance of female influence on the later Napatan royal succession.[246]

Katimala was not only effective in dealing with the enemy menace; she was also eloquent, and apparently orationally effective in her speech to the thirty chiefs. In this Katimala appears to stand near the beginning of a Third Intermediate Period tradition of eloquent women,[247] a tradition that could well correspond to an apparent general rise in the status of women during the Third Intermediate Period.[248]

Column 7 of the main inscription may contain the key to the inception of Katimala's text. When Katimala professes that one should meet out evil to those whom Amun does not know, and act kindly towards those whom Amun knows, she appears to justify her own actions in the Mountains of Gold. At the same time she implicitly condemns the failure of her predecessor. When she immediately declares that Amun "will appoint the one who is alive," she contrasts her state with that of her predecessor—her state of *ʿnḫ*-life results from trusting in Amun; the male ruler's state of *wiꜣwiꜣ*-ineptitude is then almost certainly the result of his own despair. Katimala means that the deity will appoint Katimala herself. At the time of her address to the chiefs she seems not to have taken office as ruler in her own right. Katimala's inscription is in a sense one of divine election, like the Enthronement Stela of Aspalta, although in the case of Katimala she actively presents her own selection by the god to an apparently silent group of officials, rather than quietly receiving the divinely inspired vote of a "college of electors." Katimala does not then seem to see her right to rule as part and parcel of some matriarchic society or normal female succession[249]—she is ruler not solely or even primarily because of a human standard of proper succession, or because of some political or military crisis and a resulting human alteration of succession rules—she is ruler by command of Amun as a result of her proper behavior. That proper behavior is succinctly encapsulated in her statements regarding good and evil, and trust in Amun. By virtue of her military activity Katimala fulfilled a function of the true ruler in New Kingdom Egyptian thought; whereas the male ruler was *wiꜣwiꜣ*, incapacitated, Katimala carried out the properly athletic role of the true ruler of Egypt.[250]

[246] Note the comments of Morkot, in Wenig, ed., *Studien zum antiken Sudan,* pp. 179–229; Török, in *ibid.,* pp. 273–87.

[247] See Lichtheim, *SAK* 16 (1989): 212–13, n. 9, on the eloquence of women during the Third Intermediate Period. According to Lichtheim, the quality of speaking well is apparently first directly applied to a woman in an "autobiographical" text on a statue of Shebensopdet, a granddaughter of Osorkon II (Jansen-Winkeln, *Ägyptische Biographien,* pp. 520–26 [text A13]).

[248] Note the remarks of Quirke, in Leahy and Tait, eds., *Studies on Ancient Egypt,* pp. 232–33, and his citation of Jansen-Winkeln, *BN* 71 (1994): 92–93 (who in turn cites Bates, *Eastern Libyans,* p. 108ff—one should see specifically, *ibid.,* pp. 111–14).

[249] For which see conveniently the comments and references in Lohwasser, *Die königlichen Frauen.*

[250] The proper ruler who physically takes the sword against enemies recalls the medieval European concept of the temporal ruler fulfilling a properly physical military role as the *athleta Christi*—see the comments of Ullmann, *Medieval Political Thought,* pp. 88–89.

Katimala's description of a chaotic period, and apparently a brief interregnum (the *wiꜣwiꜣ* of the male ruler), refers to events that had occurred during recent memory at the time of the inscription; in fact, her own reign has dispelled her land's misfortune. Through the use of such a *topos* of collapse, Katimala's inscription makes of her reign the introduction to a type of golden age. Like the Stele of Sethnakht from Elephantine,[251] Katimala's inscription is a historical document employing the form of the *Königsnovelle* in order to announce that the "messianic" ruler has indeed already appeared.[252] Katimala's inscription provides a bridge between earlier New Kingdom royal novels and other texts describing the resolution of a chaotic event and the later manifestations of the *Chaosbeschreibung*, such as the Demotic Chronicle and the *Oracle of the Potter*.[253]

That Katimala's inscription is not only a monument of proper royal conduct, but of the proper conduct of an important female ruler, may explain to some extent the placement of her tableau on the façade of the temple in the fortress of Semna. In the text accompanying the scene of Thutmosis III standing in front of the enthroned figure of Sesostris III on the south end of the east exterior wall of Semna Temple, Thutmosis III ordered his Nubian viceroy to renew the festival offerings of Sesostris III to the deities Dedwen and Khnum at Semna.[255] In the inscription Thutmosis III added to the earlier endowment his own offerings to two additional deities—the deified Sesostris III and that ruler's wife Queen Meretseger.[255] The apparent deification of this Twelfth Dynasty royal lady by the time of Thutmosis III evokes the slightly later deification of Amenhotep III's queen Tiye at Sedeinga, and the deification of Queen Nefertari at Abu Simbel.[256] Katimala may have located her inscription on a temple that at least to some extent honored a deified queen of the Twelfth Dynasty in anticipation of her own desired or even planned apotheosis. Curiously, although Katimala's inscription is in no way a letter to the dead, or an appeal to a deified ruler, living or dead, Egyptian or Nubian, as some have suggested, Katimala's Semna tableau may in fact be to some extent a monument of divine queenship, or more precisely a document of feminine kingship.

---

[251] Drenkhahn, *Die Elephantine-Stele des Sethnacht*; Seidlmeyer, in Gutksch and Polz, eds., *Stationen*, pp. 363–86.

[252] *Contra* the statement of Frankfurter, *Elijah in Upper Egypt*, p. 173 "apart from the literary need to contextualize a discourse with narrative, there is no intrinsic relationship between *Königsnovelle* and *Chaosbeschreibung*."

[253] Frankfurter, *Elijah in Upper Egypt*, p. 182. Of Frankfurter's catalogue of "the prophetic motifs of *Chaosbeschreibung*" (pp. 183–85), Katimala possesses most of the first category, "Chaos in Society" (a. interruption of family structure and life: strife between Katimala and her husband; b. internal social strife and rebellions: Makaresh; d. disintegration of religious cult: treatment of the sacred cattle and possible theft of temple wealth) and some of the third, "Collapse of Borders" (a. invasion of foreigners: the enemy, out of the east in general).

[254] Caminos, *Semna-Kumma* 1, pp. 41–48, pls. 24–26 (scene 11); Hofmann, *Königsnovelle*, pp. 204–8 (without reference to Caminos).

[255] For Queen Meretseger, see van Siclen, *VA* 8 (1992): 29–32 (cited by Vandersleyen, *L'Égypte et la vallée du Nil* 2, p. 87). On the deified Sesostris III in Nubia see the references in El-Nany, *BIFAO* 104/1 (2004): 207–13.

[256] See Vandersleyen, *L'Égypte et la vallée du Nil* 2, p. 376. For the deification of Tiye note also Wildung, in Freed, Markowitz, and D'Auria, eds., *Pharaohs of the Sun*, p. 215 (no. 39); Capel, in Capel and Markoe, eds., *Mistress of the House, Mistress of Heaven*, p. 112.

An Essay at Historical Interpretation

A date for Katimala's tableau in the Twenty-First or Twenty-Second Dynasty is—on the bases of iconography, palaeography, and grammar—virtually certain. Although all elements of the iconography and language of Katimala's tableau are Egyptian, nothing in the tableau supports an identification of Katimala as a daughter of any Egyptian ruler.[257] All documents of the early Third Intermdiate Period are rare in southern Upper Egypt, and in Nubia the absence of documentary material is profoundly disturbing.[258] For Katimala's tableau to be—as indeed it appears to be—the single surviving Nubian document from this period is remarkable; for the tableau to be a single, major product of an early Third Intermediate Period Egyptian foray into Nubia, with no other major or minor inscriptions of the event thus far recognized from any site to the north of Semna, is most unlikely. Although the poetic nature and psychological depth of the text leave a few points of specific information wanting, the inscription is a remarkable and thus far unique glimpse at the birth of the Napatan state, or at least the birth of one of the predecessors—perhaps the most important—of the Napatan state. Katimala defended the faith of Amun apparently a short time after the sad events at the end of the Ramesside Period.

Following a period of civil war in Egypt during the reign of the last Ramesses, Egyptian control of Nubia appears to have evaporated. Summoned to Thebes in a time of crisis, involved in a conflict with the high priest of Amun, Amenhotep—a conflict that rapidly spread throughout most if not all of Egypt—the Nubian viceroy Panehesy became a rebel leader, whom General Piankh drove back into Nubia.[259]

[257] *Contra* the rather tenuous suggestion of Bennett, *GM* 173 (1999): 7–8, that Katimala was the daughter of Osochor, and wife of Siamun (endorsed by Kendall, in Wenig, ed., *Studien zum antiken Sudan,* pp. 59–63; Edwards, *The Nubian Past,* p. 117).

[258] Compare the remarks of Peden, *Graffiti,* p. 277, who notes that rock inscriptions of Dynasties Twenty-One to Twenty-Five are rare at Aswan; no rock inscriptions firmly dated to this period are thus far known from Nubia. According to Adams, in Sasson, ed., *Civilizations of the Ancient Near East* 1, p. 779, expressing what appears to be a common sentiment: "What happened in Kush immediately after the Egyptian departure is not known, for there are neither textual nor archaeological records."

[259] See Jansen-Winkeln, *ZÄS* 119 (1992): 22–26; *idem, ZÄS* 122 (1995): 62–78; see also Niwiński, *BIFAO* 95 (1995): 329–60, for a defense of a slightly different interpretation of the events (on p. 337 he interestingly suggests that: "Il est possible que Panehsy, en menant à la lutte son armée constituée de Nubiens, ait exploité l'idée de libérer la Nubie de la domination égyptienne").

While the Egypt of the Twenty-First Dynasty turned in upon herself, cannibalizing the tombs of her own recently deceased royal dead in order to compensate for the products of foreign trade and the fruits of military adventure no longer flowing into the country as they once did, Nubia appears to have suffered from foreign raids. Although Panehesy may have been buried in his tomb at Aniba,[260] the office of the Viceroy of Kush may have become more a titular sign of royal favor and an economic boon linked to the surviving viceregal holdings north of Aswan. Rather than any surviving Nubian temples controlling the mining regions in the stead of the Egyptians, Katimala's Semna inscription suggests that desert dwellers made life difficult for the remaining adherents of the cult of Amun in Nubia. During the Twenty-First Dynasty in Egypt, the high priest of Amun of Karnak, Menkheperre, attempted to re-establish a Theban based Egyptian hegemony over the oases of the Western Desert, and constructed fortresses at the ends of a number of important desert roads leading in and out of the Nile Valley.[261] He appears not to have attempted to reestablish any direct Egyptian control over Nubia, and for the entire Twenty-First Dynasty the only evidence of possible Nubian ties are the *imy(.t)-r ḫꜣs.wt rsy.wt*, "Superintendent of Southern Foreign Lands," and *sꜣ.t-nsw.t n Kš*, "Viceroy of Kush." titles of Neskhons, wife of Pinudjem II.[262] Three further viceroys appear in documents of the Third Intermediate Period, one from the reign of Osorkon II, another probably from the reign of Takelot II, and another not as yet assignable to a particular reign,[263] but these titles are not matched by any documentary or archaeological evidence that their holders might actually have exercised any real authority south of Aswan.

Although Lower Nubia in particular is often supposed to have been at best thinly populated from about 1100–750 BCE,[264] such a condition is much to be doubted,[265] and probably results from a misreading of the available archaeological record.[266] Settlements in Lower Nubia may have dwindled in favor of a nomadic or semi-nomadic lifestyle, although—in spite of the probable abandonment of most of the earlier temples—some vestiges of urban life may have continued.[267] The presence of the

[260] Steindorff, *Aniba* 2, pp. 240–41 and pl. 29c, published the apparent tomb of Panehesy, tomb SA 38.

[261] Kitchen, *Third Intermediate Period,* pp. 249 and 269–70; Darnell, in Friedman, ed., *Egypt and Nubia,* pp. 132–35.

[262] Kitchen, *Third Intermediate Period,* p. 358, §320 n. 663; *ibid.,* pp. 275–76, §232, Kitchen discusses Neskhons, noting that she was a prophetess of Nebethetepet Lady of Sered (Kitchen suggests this may be a Nubian toponym). See also Kees, *Priestertum,* pp. 165–66; Naguib, *Le clergé féminin,* p. 169. Was this in fact "to keep her claim to revenues of this office coming from domains in Upper Egypt"? –so Habachi, *Lexikon der Ägyptologie* 3, col. 635; see also Winand, *Karnak* 11 (Paris, 2003), p. 651 n. j.

[263] See Zibelius-Chen, *SAK* 16 (1989): 338 and 340, and the references cited there.

[264] Compare the remarks of Edwards, *The Nubian Past,* p. 128; Redford, *From Slave to Pharaoh,* pp. 58–59.

[265] Compare the remarks of De Simone, in Barich and Gatto, eds., *Dynamics of Populations,* pp. 123–24.

[266] See the remarks and references of Heidorn, *Fortress of Dorginarti,* pp. 102–3; Williams, *Twenty-Fifth Dynasty and Napatan Remains at Quatul,* p. 44.

[267] For the collapse of the earlier temples compare the remarks of Welsby, *Kingdom of Kush,* pp. 72–73. Török sees the "el Kurru chiefdom" as the true precursor of the Twenty-Fifth Dynasty, and proposes a collapse, but not a depopulation, of the Egyptianizing "temple-towns" of Nubia.

Katimala inscription at Semna, if her inscription does in fact date to the time of the early Third Intermediate Period in Egypt, suggests strongly that a rather contracted representation of Napatan occupation around Gebel Barkal and from Shaqadud to Meroe[268] is incorrect. The presence of a *šmsy.t Mwt* following the queen, and the accurate iconography of that figure when compared to images from Third Intermediate Period Egypt, also suggests that a cult of Amun in contact with the Theban center of that cult flourished in Nubia during the time of the Twenty-First Dynasty. Neskhons title of "Viceroy of Kush" might well indicate a Theban spiritual hegemony over surviving priesthoods in Nubia.[269]

The historical information in Katimala's inscription is modest, but one may nevertheless find some indications regarding the general conditions in Lower Nubia during the early first millennium BCE. The inscription begins with an address by a male ruler—perhaps a king, in any event a man to whom the inscription refers as *ḥm=f*—to Queen Katimala. His statement and the queen's subsequent speech suggest that the king at the time of his address to Katimala had just returned in defeat from some encounter with a seemingly inexorable foe. The two virtual relatives dependent upon *ḫfty* in column 2 express a state of continuous warfare between the Kushite state during (and perhaps even before) the time of Katimala and some enemy power, neither group being able to deliver a decisive blow to the other.

The "event of the year," the *md.t rnp.t*, is perhaps synonymous with the *ỉꜣd.t rnp.t*, the potentially evil influences of the New Year.[270] The king's speech and the queen's initial statement together recall a portion of the Words of Khakheperresoneb, specifically the section beginning BM EA 5645 recto 10–11:[271]

ink pw ḥr nkꜣy m ḫpr.t
　　sḫr.w ḫpr ḫt tꜣ
ḫprw.w ḥr ḫpr
　　nn mi snf
dns rnp.t r sn.nwt=s

"I am meditating on what has happened,
　　the state of things that have happened throughout the land;
changes are happening—
　　it is not like last year.
Each year is more burdensome than its fellow."[272]

---

[268] As in Sadr, *Development of Nomadism*, p. 112.

[269] As Niwiński, *BIFAO* 95 (1995): 348, suggested.

[270] On which see Bergman, *Isis-Seele und Osiris-Ei*, pp. 45–48; Germond, Sekhmet et la protection du monde, pp. 286–304; Goyon, *BIFAO* 74 (1974): 77–83; Derchain, *Les Monuments religieux à l'entrée de l'Ouady Helal*, pp. 58–59 (n. 36); etc.; compare also Hannig, *Ägyptisches Wörterbuch I, Altes Reich und Erste Zwischenzeit*, p. 578.

[271] Gardiner, *Admonitions of an Egyptian Sage*, pl. 17; Kadish, *JEA* 59 (1973): pl. 32; Parkinson, *JEA* 83 (1997): 56, l. 15–58, l. 2, and pls. 10 and 12.

[272] Translation of Parkinson, *The Tale of Sinuhe*, p. 147, here graphically arranged to mirror the grammatical structure of the transliteration.

Although not as direct as other quotations in the corpus of Napatan historical texts,[273] the emphasis on the *md.t rnp.t* in Katimala's inscriptions may well allude to the Words of Khakheperresoneb, or to a related text. According to the Enthronement Stela of Aspelta and the Stela of Excommunication, the *md.t*-affair that is evil is a matter performed in ignorance of Amun, without the deity.[274] In comparison with the Words of Khakheperresoneb, the queen concludes the section of her text in question with a denial of such a worry as begins BM 5645 recto.

What is the event, or were there in fact multiple deeds of evil? The theft of gold and silver to which the inscription refers (ll. 2 and 3) may relate specifically to the robbery of temple treasures made of those precious metals, although together "gold and silver" may encompass all valuables in general.[275] One aspect of the robbery may have involved the closing off of the gold mining regions of the Eastern Desert, for Katimala appears to refer to the place of her victory as the "mountains of gold" (l. 4), probably an allusion to the area of the old "Gold of Wawat."

The location of Katimala's inscription at the southern end of the Second Cataract, and her reference to fighting an enemy in the mountains of gold together suggest that Katimala was interested in securing control of both Nilotic and Eastern Desert routes, and she may also have desired to control the middle portion of the Western Desert routes passing through the small oases of Bir Nakhlai, Shebb, and Selima.[276] The locations of many Napatan sites at land and river trade route termini show trade, specifically in gold to the north and iron to the south, to have been integral to the Napatan state.[277] East of the Nile and north of Meroe were apparently the hostile Rehrehes, the apparently equally hostile Meded perhaps being west thereof,[278] and the land of Shabet that bedeviled Harsiotef as well may also be a region washed by the Red Sea.[279] One or more of those groups may represent the descendents of the enemies who so bedeviled Katimala's predecessor, and against whom Katimala was forced to take up arms. The difficulties of more modern and mechanized military forces campaigning in the region of the Nubian Eastern Desert,[280] and the war-like zeal with which many

[273] Compare those collected by Jasnow, in Teeter and Larson, eds., *Gold of Praise,* pp. 193–210.

[274] Grimal, *Quatre stèles napatéennes,* pp. 27, ll. 8–10, 28, ll. 8–10, and 29, l. 5 (Enthronement Stela ll. 12, 14, and 16), and p. 38, ll. 9–14 (Stela of Excommunication ll. 5–7).

[275] Compare the remarks of Aufrère, *L'Univers mineral 2,* p. 420. For silver alone as a designation of "money" or "payment" see Janssen, *Commodity Prices,* pp. 499–501.

[276] Gleichen, *The Anglo-Egyptian Sudan* 1, pp. 25–26 and 202–3 (and the map at the back, showing routes leaving the Nile from Sagiet el-Abd, south of the Second Cataract, for Selima, and leaving the Nile near Wadi Halfa for Bir Nakhlai and Shebb); *ibid.*, 2, pp. 167 and 192; see also Thiry, *Le Sahara libyen,* p. 404.

[277] Sadr, *Nomadism,* p. 113.

[278] Stela of Harsiotef: see Grimal, *Quatre stèles napatéennes,* p. 51, ll. 4–10 (campaign against the Rehrehes); p. 51, ll. 12–15 (campaign against the Meded); pp. 52–53 (two further campaigns against the Meded); p. 55, l.5–p. 56, l. 16 (two further campaigns against the Rehrehes); Macadam, *Kawa* 1, pp. 45–46.

[279] Stela of Harsiotef: Grimal, *Quatre stèles napatéennes,* p. 44, ll. 9–13; for *Šꜣb.t* see Posener, *Première Domination perse,* p. 62 n. 3; Edel, *Or.* 40 (1971): 7 and 9.

[280] See conveniently Robson, *Fuzzy Wuzzy,* and the references cited there. For a description of the Etbai region, in which Katimala may have encountered her enemies, see Gleichen, ed., *Anglo-Egyptian Sudan* 1, pp. 85–90.

of the groups inhabiting the southern Etbai have sought to maintain their rapacious and independent lifestyle,[281] reveal that the tone of crisis that hangs about Katimala's inscription is probably a true echo of what may have been savage desert fighting at the dawn of the Napatan state.

In Nubia, after about one and a half centuries of seemingly independent existence following the rebellion of Panehesy, Shoshenq I may have initiated some sort of military activity in Nubia.[282] No direct evidence for any substantial trade, or even any specific, unstereotyped reference to Egyptian activity in Nubian is, however, forthcoming for the reign of Sheshonq I.[283] Osorkon I may also have employed Nubian troops, and perhaps a Nubian general served him as well,[284] but still no direct evidence is forthcoming of any considerable Egyptian activity in Nubia, or interference with Nubian affairs, during the Twenty-First and Twenty-Second Dynasties.[285]

Although some wars marred the relative peace of New Kingdom Nubia, the riverine and desert elements of Nubia appear to have coexisted with little apparent conflict.

---

281 Compare the remarks of Paul, *The Beja,* pp. 1–11 *et passim.* If the reference to some offence to the cattle of Amun is indeed an allusion to difficulties with the herds of the Amun domain, dwellers in the Eastern Desert might well be responsible, for they have a long history of cattle rustling—compare the remarks of Russell Pasha, *Egyptian Service,* pp. 56–57. For discussions of the apparent conflicts between the dwellers in the highlands and those in the lowlands in the Mediterranean world, see the references in Horden and Purcell, *Corrupting Sea,* p. 551.

282 Kitchen, *Third Intermediate Period,* p. 293 n. 284, cites Epigraphic Survey, *Reliefs and Inscriptions at Karnak* 3, pls. 3 and 5, l. 6: *iw ptpt.n=k iwnty.w-sty,* "you have trampled the Nubians." Note also the label to the scene: *sḳr wr.w iwn.tyw-sty.w ḫꜣs.wt nb.w(t) štꜣ.(w)t tꜣ.w nb.w Fnḫw ḫꜣs.wt pḥw.w Stt,* "Smiting the chiefs of the Nubian nomads, all the distant foreign lands, all the lands of the Fenekhu, the *pḥw.w*-regions of Asia." The king grasps a great bundle of enemies, seventeen bearded heads—Asiatics?—and two Nubian heads to each side. Note also the reference to Kushite elements in the army Sheshonq I led into Syro-Palestine, according to 2 Chronicles 12: 3–4, although these could be the result of military conquest or mercenary enlistment (see Kitchen, *Third Intermediate Period,* pp. 295–96).

283 Blocks from Karnak, assigned initially to the reign of Sheshonq I (Müller, *Egyptological Researches* 2, pp. 143–53; Kitchen, *Third Intermediate Period,* p. 293, §251), actually belong to Taharqa (*ibid.,* p. 575, §509). Kendall, in Wenig, ed., *Studien zum antiken Sudan,* p. 51, in a paper presented in 1992 and published in 1999, refers to Kitchen's original (1973) belief that the Taharqa blocks date to the reign of Sheshonq I, not to Vernus' study (1975) or Kitchen's later correction (1986), and thereby suggests that the reign of Sheshonq I may attest to direct Egyptian diplomatic and military activity in Nubia (so also O'Connor, in Trigger, Kemp, O'Connor, and Lloyd, *Ancient Egypt,* p. 268). Török, *Kingdom of Kush,* p. 109, n. 193, also accepts a Nubian campaign of Sheshonq I as "probable." Morkot, in Wenig, ed., *Studien zum antiken Sudan,* pp. 143–144, recognized that the Karnak blocks are not evidence for Sheshonq I in Nubia, and any campaign assigned to that ruler is based on assumption, and the modest and unspecific information from Sheshonq's victory scene at the Bubastite Portal of Karnak (see preceding note).

284 Schulman, in *Studies Simpson* 2, pp. 713–15, suggests that the possible Kushite general Zerah, under Osorkon I (II Chronicles 14: 8–13 and 16: 8–9), may be a Western Asiatic.

285 Török, *Birth of an Ancient African Kingdom,* pp. 20–23, unconvincingly suggests that certain traditional royal epithets of the Twenty-First and Twenty-Second Dynasties (such as the *Nb.ty* name of Smendes I and the titulary of Psusennes I) refer in some way to military activity in Nubia; in this he follows to some extent remarks of Zibelius-Chen, *SAK* 16 (1989): 334–37 *et passim.* The epithets in fact do not provide evidence of specific activity in Nubia.

This peaceful tradition changed rapidly after the end of the Ramesside Period, and Katimala appears to have inherited a fragmented society in which the dwellers on the Nile and those in the Eastern Desert found themselves in conflict. The strife between the followers of Amun and the marauders from the desert that forms the background to Katimala's inscription may to some extent be the result of an arid period at the end of the second millennium BCE.[286] The loss of some agricultural land near the Nile may have led the riverine groups, the vestiges of New Kingdom urban society, to establish seasonal grazing stations away from the Nile, in order to preserve as much of the increasingly precious riparian land as possible for agriculture. At the same time, the increased aridity would probably have lured groups once more self-sufficiently ensconced in the desert hinterlands to venture at least periodically into the Nile Valley. Such adaptations to periods of increased aridity in already arid environments are documented in more recent times,[287] and could explain the strife in Katimala's reign.

The conflict Katimala's inscription so vaguely describes took place in the mountains of gold. The location of her inscription at Semna suggests that the struggles in the mountains of gold may have been centered north of Abu Hamed and east of Amara, in the region of the "Gold of Wawat," perhaps in and around the Wadi Gabgaba and the Wadi Allaqi in the Eastern Desert. The extension of Napatan control to the region of Semna would also secure the "Gold of Kush" near the Nile between Kerma and Buhen.[288] Sites of immediate post-New Kingdom gold production are sparse in the recognized archaeological record, but those thus far recognized suggest a minimal resumption, if not continuation, of gold production in roughly the same areas.[289] As the mining of gold in the Egyptian Eastern Desert appears to have ceased at the end of the Ramesside Period, not to be resumed until the Ptolemaic Period,[290] securing and reopening or even continuing unabated the mining of gold in Nubia would provide a powerful advantage to the nascent Napatan State in dealings with its northern neighbor. Tombs at Hillat el-Arab, near Gebel Barkal, appear to show that immediately post-New Kingdom Nubia was wealthier than she was under the last of the Ramesside viceroys.[291] The probable source of this wealth, the mountains of gold of the Nubian Eastern Desert and the goods that gold bought, attracted the enemy chief who stole from the state of Katimala's predecessor.

---

[286] Compare Welsby, Macklin, and Woodward, in Friedman, ed., *Egypt and Nubia,* pp. 36–37; Edwards in Welsby, ed., *Recent Research in Kushite History and Archaeology,* pp. 69–70; *idem, The Nubian Past,* p. 109.

[287] Horne, in Cameron and Tomka, eds., *Abandonment of settlements and regions,* pp. 43–53.

[288] See Vercoutter, *Kush* 7 (1959): 120–53; Castiglioni, Castiglioni and Vercoutter, *Das Goldland der Pharaonen,* pp. 18, 27, and 112.

[289] See Klemm, Klemm, and Murr, in Friedman, ed., *Egypt and Nubia,* p. 226, fig. 5 (compare also the maps p. 225, fig. 4, and p. 229, fig. 8). *Ibid.,* p. 218 they describe evidence for reuse of New Kingdom stone mills, apparently during the post-Ramesside Period, and indicate the potential of future work at such sites for providing more accurate evidence on the date and extent of the resumption of gold mining in Nubia. See also Klemm and Klemm, *Nürnberger Blätter zur Archäologie* 13 (1997): 149–66.

[290] *Ibid.,* p. 218 (and the chart p. 231, fig. 10); Klemm and Klemm, *MDAIK* 50 (1994): 189–222.

[291] See Liverani, in Welsby and Anderson, eds., *Sudan,* pp. 138–40.

Katimala and her realm began as an embattled enclave in the Nile Valley. In the end Katimala asked if it were not right to make a land for Amun, where there was not formerly his place. The implication of the queen's question is that the outcome of her war would be the "Amunization" of the Eastern Desert, the conversion of the tribes there and their subsequent inclusion in the nascent Napatan realm. These deductions from Katimala's inscription suggest that Adam's reconstruction of the origin of the Napatan kingdom—alliance between the priesthood of Amun at Gebel Barkal and the leaders of surrounding desert tribes—may well be accurate.[292] Whether the queen's name is read *Kꜣtymꜣlw* or *Kꜣrymꜣlw*, if the apparent Meroitic nature of that name is indeed correct, then through her own name Katimala may also reveal some union between a northern Nubian kingdom, centered around el-Kurru and perhaps Gebel Barkal, already allied with if not even including the Butana.[293] That she placed her inscription on the façade of the temple at Semna reveals a use of that temple, and perhaps the establishment or at least specific patronage of a cult and associated urban center at Semna. That Katimala chose the old temple is not necessarily a symbol of weakness, but may well represent a conscious effort to reestablish what appears to have been a fading urbanism in Lower Nubia, strengthening her own position more through the creation of an urban family, tying together the family groups inhabiting the site than through the rebuilding or raising of the old fortification walls.[294]

As the inscription of Katimala appears to date to the early first millennium BCE, the Semna tableau does not seem destined to bring any new evidence to bear on the arguments between the long and short chronologies for the el-Kurru cemetery. Because of her relatively early date, however, Katimala and her Semna inscription do have a direct bearing on the discussion of the el-Kurru royal cemetery, the earliest tombs of which appear to date to some time around the middle of the ninth century BCE,[295] approximately a century after the time of Katimala. If, as seems likely, the el-Kurru tombs are the sepulchers of the line of local rulers out of which the Twenty-Fifth Dynasty emerged, then the relatively primitive nature of the Generation A burials at el-Kurru suggest that those rulers were themselves perhaps not the direct descendents of Katimala. Katimala's tableau at least strongly implies that somewhere in Lower Nubia, probably in the region of the Second Cataract, Nubian rulers were continuing and even developing an Egypto-Nubian state centered on the worship of the god Amun during the apparent dark age between the end of the Ramesside Period and the rise of the dynasty of el-Kurru. The el-Kurru dynasts may not themselves have rediscovered

[292] See Sadr, *The Development of Nomadism,* p. 111.

[293] Török, *Kingdom of Kush,* pp. 129–30 suggests that Katimala's name indicates the union of Kush and the Meroitic-speaking Butana "was reinforced by the intermarriage of the el Kurru dynasty and the family of the local princes." Note also *idem, Birth of an Ancient African Kingdom,* p. 45.

[294] Compare amongst others the remarks of Hull, *African Cities and Towns,* pp. 92–93.

[295] For the lively debate concerning the nature and date of the earliest of the el-Kurru royal tombs, see Morkot, in Wenig, ed., *Studien zum antiken Sudan,* pp. 10–31, 44–47, and 49–78; Török, in *ibid.,* pp. 149–58; and the response in Kendall, in *ibid.,* pp. 164–74; see also Heidorn, *JARCE* 31 (1994): 115–31, a work important in supporting the apparently superior "short chronology" which Kendall advocates.

and reinvented a peculiarly Nubian version of the pharaonic state, but they may in fact have been the descendents and even the pupils of a shadowy precursor state, the kingdom over which Katimala held sway.[296] The burials of Katimala, her predecessor, and any others of her as yet shadowy "dynasty," may yet lie hidden in Nubia.[297]

Katimala's inscription appeals to her supporters to identify themselves with true and loyal servants of Amun, following her example, and to oppose actively the unbelieving enemy. The Semna tableau appears to be part of an attempt to create an "origin myth" for the Napatan State—at least the state Katimala seems to have hoped to found—an origin based on a "crusade" of the followers of Amun against the "heathen."[298] Katimala clearly seeks to provide a causal link between her own faith in Amun and loyalty to his cult, and the military defeat of those who did not trust in Amun. Her success impels those who would themselves succeed to follow her example of ritual purity, even to spread abroad this ritual purity and literally make lands anew for Amun.[299] Katimala's view of divinely sanctioned warfare is well founded in Egyptian—a deity (for the New Kingdom and the early Third Intermediate Period at least the warring deity *par excellence* was Amun) gave victory; in their songs of praise military contingents in festivals would clearly state: "Amun is the god who decrees it—victory be to the ruler!"[300] Although the evidence of the later el-Kurru royal tombs may not reveal a definite impact of Egyptian religious thought and clerical authority on the burial practices of the nascent Napatan state,[301] Katimala's inscription reveals already, shortly after the end of the Ramesside Period, the overwhelming legitimizing importance of the cult of Amun for the independent rulers of first millennium Nubia.

Katimala invokes the concept of a just war. She is careful, however, not merely to ascribe to Amun the responsibility for the military activity, and to promise to him a geographical offering as a result. She also appeals to the historical failure of her predecessor as a means of legitimizing her own rule. Her reference to the mountains of gold also suggests a nod to the importance of mammon to the well-founded Napatan state. Though in medieval European crusading the two concepts of holy war and just war, the religious exaltation and the legal limitation of war, may not have mingled fully until well within, if not at the very end, of the first century of Europe's forays

[296] Katimala may have belonged even to a state or one might perhaps more accurately suggest a family who coexisted or even competed with the direct precursors to the el-Kurru rulers—compare the remarks of Morkot, *CRIPEL* 17 (1995): 237.

[297] Note Edwards, *The Nubian Past,* p. 120, who states—when discussing the el-Kurru burials—"That other early elite burials await discovery elsewhere also seems very likely."

[298] For a similar use of crusading imagery to enhance political legitimation, see the remarks of Sieber-Lehmann, in Housley, ed., *Crusading in the Fifteenth Century,* pp. 81–83.

[299] For ritual purity and the Egyptians' concepts of history during the first millennium BCE, see the remarks of Loprieno, in Tait, ed., *'Never Had the Like Occurred',* pp. 146–48.

[300] Compare the Epigraphic Survey, *Reliefs and Inscriptions at Luxor Temple* 1, pl. 91, ll. 1 and 2, and p. 35 n. *a* to that plate, and pl. 123, fragment 1245, and p. 45 n. *a* to that fragment; Manassa, *Great Karnak Inscription of Merneptah,* p. 127, n. *e*.

[301] Compare the remarks of Yellin, *CRIPEL* 17/1 (1995): 244–48 and 257.

into Syro-Palestine,[302] Katimala had already both promulgated, led, and reported on her own just and holy conflict.

Katimala in some ways seems to follow the tradition of Ramesses II at the battle of Kadesh, calling upon Amun and appealing to the power of personal piety to overcome the enemy. At the same time Katimala innovates in that she appears to advocate a forgetting of the past; she does not bargain with the deity in her text, nor does she seem to countenance any great search for historical precedent. Her statement that she did not remember the past events, but trusted in Amun, encapsulates her apparent desire to fire her supporters with devotion, and at the same time to make of her reign by default a new beginning, a true *sp tpy* for the Napatan State.[303]

Katimala appears to have viewed her war—or at least she desired that the readers of her inscription should so view her war—as a struggle between the faithful servants of Amun against enemies of the deity. She also suggests that her success following failure was success born of blind trust in Amun, following a ruler who was troubled by the malevolent events that had assailed his reign. In face of the failure of doubt and the attack of the unbelieving, for Katimala only the most fervent devotion to Amun could bring victory. In the face of this intense personal reliance on faith in Amun, Piye's concern that his troops be ritually pure before entering the precinct of Karnak becomes something more than good manners and political sagacity. Piye is indeed in many ways similar to the conquistadors of a much more recent period—hardened in the forge of local and perhaps even fratricidal war, and fired by a religious fervor that casts their enemies in the role of the minions of unbelieving opponents of the cosmic order, and certain that right and divinity are on their side, they expand the horizons of their conflict, and bring fire, sword, and militant religiosity far beyond the confines of their homeland.

[302] See Cowdrey, in Bull and Housley, eds., *Experience of Crusading* 1, pp. 175–92, and the references cited there.

[303] Edwards, *Nubian Past,* p. 116, discusses Alara's dedication of his sister to the Amun cult, and says that "what is not known, of course, is the extent to which the Amun cult, and other 'Egyptian' cults may have been established parts of religious practice in the region during the New Kingdom and later periods, or indeed how they might relate to 'indigeous beliefs." Katimala's inscription seems to go some way to remedying this apparent gap in our knowledge."

The Main Inscription — Continuous Transliteration and Translation

Part 1: Introduction—the complaint of a ruler to Katimala

TRANSLITERATION:

[1]ḥsb.t 14 <ꜣbd> 2 pr.t sw 9
ḏd ỉn ḥm=f n ḥm.t nsw.t wr.t sꜣ.t nsw.t Kꜣtimꜣlw mꜣꜥ.tỉ-ḫrw

twnn <r> tnw
ỉw bn twnn bꜣky m-ẖnw nꜣ bꜣk.w n ỉmn
ỉw wn [2]ḫfty
ỉw mn dỉ(=i) ḫpr tꜣ md.t n tꜣ rnp.t ỉḫpr.t n=n
ỉw mn dỉ(=i) ḫpr=s ỉrr=w b(i)n
ỉw mn dỉ(=i) ḫpr n=n
ỉw wn wr
ỉw ꜥw(ꜣi)=f nbw ḥḏ
mtw=f ỉr ỉmn n ⸢wꜥꜣ⸣ [3]ṯny ỉm=i
ḫfty ⸢rwi⸣

VARIANT TRANSLITERATION:

twnn <r> tnw
ỉw bn twnn bꜣky m-ẖnw nꜣ bꜣk.w n ỉmn
ỉw wn [2]ḫfty(.w)
ỉw mn=w (ḥr) dỉ(.t) ḫpr tꜣ md.t n tꜣ rnp.t ỉḫpr.t n=n
ỉw mn=w (ḥr) dỉ(.t) ḫpr=s ỉrr=w
ỉw bn mn=w (ḥr) dỉ(.t) ḫpr n=n
ỉw wn wr
ỉw diw=f nbw ḥḏ
mtw=f ỉr ỉmn n ⸢biꜣ⸣

Part 2: The Queen Responds

TRANSLITERATION:

[3]ỉry bꜣk n ỉmn p3 ỉrw=ỉ
ỉw bwpw=ỉ sḫꜣy tꜣ md.t ỉḫpr r=ỉ m tꜣ rnp.t
m-ḏr hꜣn=ỉ n ỉmn
ỉꜣd ꜥwꜣ nbw(?) ḥḏ

pꜣ [4]dỉw n(ꜣ)y=ỉ ỉt.w ỉšsp=[i] n=w sỉn n=ỉ
m-ḫt wywy=f
ỉw=ỉ ỉr=f m ḏw.w nbw

ḫr ỉ.ỉr=ỉ ꜥm m tꜣ rnp.t
ỉꜣy nḫt ḥkꜣy pꜣ nṯr

Part 1: Introduction—the complaint of a ruler to Katimala

TRANSLATION:

[1]Year 14, <month> 2 of the Peret Season, day 9:
Speech by his majesty to the king's great wife and the daughter of the king, Katimala, vindicated:

"Whither are we (to turn)
if we do not serve among the servants of Amun?
when there is an [2]opponent;
otherwise will occur the annual thing that occurs to us;
otherwise it will go badly for them (scil. the servants of Amun);
otherwise (it) will happen to us;
when there is a chieftain
who has robbed gold and silver,
and always treated Amun as ⸢accursed⸣—who exaulted me.
The enemy ⸢escaped.⸣"

VARIANT TRANSLATION:

Whither are we (to turn)
if we do not serve among the servants of Amun?
when there are [2]enemies;
who continue causing to happen the annual thing that occurs to us;
and to whom I continue to cause that it happen;
but they will not continue causing that (it) happen to us;
for there is a chieftain,
who has given gold and silver,
and treated Amun marvelously.

Part 2: The Queen Responds

TRANSLATION:

[3]"What I did was to act as servant of Amun.
for I did not remember the event which happened to me this year,
since I have trusted in Amun,
who attacks him who robbed [gold and] ⸢silver⸣.

[4]He whom my fathers—to whom [I] have succeeded—appointed hastened to me,
after he had failed/become physically disabled;
and I did it in the mountains of gold;

For it was that year I achieved the understanding—
then powerful is the magic of god.

Part 3: The Queen Addresses a Council of Chiefs—Fear is the Enemy

TRANSLITERATION:

ḫr ḏd=ỉ [5]*<n> 30 n wr.w n(?)* [...]

bỉn pꜣ Pr-ꜥꜣ ḳḳ m ḫpš=f

ỉs.tw nfr snḏ ỉrm ḫꜣꜥ pḥ.wy r-ḥꜣ.t ḫrwy
mỉ ḳd pꜣ wn nꜣy(=ỉ) ⸢ỉt.w⸣ [5-6]*ỉšsp(=ỉ)* [6]*n=w <ḥr> ỉr(.t)=f*

ḫr ỉỉr ... tꜣ rnp.t ḥr tꜣ md.t ỉḫpr ỉr=ỉ

ḫr ỉr nꜣy(=i) ỉt.w ỉwn ssnḏ nꜣ ḫrwy.w nb(.w)
wn=w ḥms
ỉw=w nfr ỉ[rm nꜣy]=w ḥm.wt

Part 4: The Queen Addresses a Council of Chiefs—What is Good and What is Bad

TRANSLITERATION:

[7]*nfr ỉry bỉn m-dỉ pꜣ ⸢nty⸣ bw ỉr=f ꜥm ỉm=f*
bỉn ỉry bỉn m-dỉ rḫy(.t) ỉw=f ꜥm

ỉw=f r dỉ.t pꜣ nty ꜥnḫ
ptr n=n ⸢my⸣ [sḏm=n(?)] [n]ꜣy bỉn
[8]*ỉw=w ꜥnḫ*

bỉn ỉry nfr
ꜥḏꜣ pꜣ ḏd ⸢nṯr⸣

ỉrw iỉr ꜥnḫ
ỉry nfr

Part 5: The Queen Addresses a Council of Chiefs—Make Unto Amun New Lands

TRANSLITERATION:

ỉs.tw nfr ỉr n ỉmn kꜣyw tꜣ(.w)
ỉw bn tꜣy=f s.t ỉwnꜣ

ḫr ỉr pꜣ nty <ḥr> ỉr <n> ỉmn ktỉ s.t
ḫr ⸢ptr⸣ ... šꜣꜥ [9]*pꜣ hrw*
ỉw ns-sw hy [n]ꜣy=ỉ ỉt

Part 3: The Queen Addresses a Council of Chiefs—Fear is the Enemy

Translation:

And I said [5]<to> 30 of the chiefs of(?)...

'Bad is the pharaoh who is stripped of his strength.

Is it good to fear, and to show the back before the enemy,
as did (my) ⸢fathers⸣ [6]to whom [5-6](I) succeeded?

Since it was because of the event that occurred to me that ... did ... in that year.

Now as for (my) fathers who were wont to frighten all the enemies,
they dwelled
happily with their wives.

Part 4: The Queen Addresses a Council of Chiefs—What is Good and What is Bad

Translation:

[7]It is good to do evil to this one whom he does not know;
it is bad to do evil to people whom he knows.

He shall appoint the one who is alive.
See here—[we have heard(?)] ⸢these⸣ evil ones,
[8]while they were yet alive—

"It is bad to do good.
That which [god] said is false."

Do what makes life—
Do good.

Part 5: The Queen Addresses a Council of Chiefs—Make Unto Amun New Lands

Translation:

Is it not good to do/make other lands for Amun,
where there is not his place?

For as for the one who makes <for> Amun another place—
Look, he will ... down to today,
he (indefinite) belonging to the annals of my fathers.

Part 6: The Queen Addresses a Council of Chiefs—the Cattle of Amun

Transliteration:

ỉs.tw bỉn ḫrp tꜣy ḫrpw n ỉmn m mn.t
nfr šꜥ.t n tꜣ ḫrpw n ỉmn mỉ ḳd pꜣ [*iir*] [9–10]*Mkꜣrš*
[10]*ỉw ỉỉr nꜣ n rmṯ nb n nỉw.t sḥwr Mkꜣršꜣ m mn.t*
ỉw dmy n=f mỉ ḳd ꜥḏn
ỉw bw-pwy … =f

[10–11]*bỉn* [11]*pḥww r-ḥꜣ.t=f*
mỉ-ḳd pꜣ [*n*]*ty* <*ḥr*> *pḥw r-ḥꜣ.t pꜣ mšꜥ pꜣ ỉr nfr n tꜣ ḏr=f*
bỉn ỉr n=f pꜣ nty … …

Part 7: The Fragmentary Conclusion

Transliteration:

… ꜥꜣ(?) *ptpt … rẖ.*[*k*?]*wỉ*
ỉw=ỉ ỉr w(?) *…*
… r=ỉ mỉ-ḳd
rn=ỉ(?) *ỉỉrw*(?) *…*
rn=⸢*k*⸣(?) *iir*(?) *…*

Part 6: The Queen Addresses a Council of Chiefs—the Cattle of Amun

Translation:

Is it bad to control this cattle of Amun daily?
Is it good to sacrifice from the herd of Amun, like that [which] [9–10]Makaresh [did]?
[10]since daily all the city people cursed Makaresh,
while there afflicted him likewise destruction,
[...] not having done(?) [...]

[10–11]Is it evil [11]to flee before him,
like the one who flees before the army of the one who does good for the entire land?
Evil is doing for him that which ...

Part 7: The Fragmentary Conclusion

Translation:

... trampling ... I know,
while I act ...
... against/toward me, entirely.
It is my reputation (?) that has made(?) ...
It is ⸢your⸣ reputation(?) that has made(?) ...

Bibliography

Adams, William Y. "The Kingdom and Civilization of Kush in Northeast Africa," in J.M. Sasson, ed., *Civilizations of the Ancient Near East,* 2 vols. (Peabody, MA: Hendrickson, 2000), pp. 775–87.

Andrews, Carol. *Amulets of Ancient Egypt* (London: British Museum Press, 1994).

Assmann, Jan. "Eine Traumoffenbarung der Göttin Hathor," *RdÉ* 30 (1978): 22–50.

Aufrère, Sydney. *L'Univers mineral dans la pensée égyptienne,* 2 vols., BdÉ 105 (Cairo: Institut Français d'Archéologie Orientale, 1991).

Baer, Klaus. "Ein Grab Verfluchen?," *Orientalia* 34 (1965): 428–38.

Bakr, Mohamed I. "Amon, der Herdenstier," *ZÄS* 98 (1970): 1–4.

Barns, John W. *Five Ramesseum Papyri* (Oxford: Griffith Institute, 1956).

———. "A New Wisdom Text from a Writing-Board in Oxford," *JEA* 54 (1968): 71–76.

Bates, Oric. *The Eastern Libyans, an Essay* (London: Macmillan, 1924).

Bechhaus-Gerst, M. "Sprachliche und historische Rekonstruktionen im Bereich des Nubischen unter besonderer Berücksichtigung des Nilnubischen," *SUGIA—Sprache und Geschichte in Afrika* 6 (1984/85): 7–134.

Beckerath, Jürgen von. "Die «Stele der Verbannten» im Museum des Louvre," *RdEÉ* 20 (1968): 7–36.

Bell, Lanny. "Luxor Temple and the Cult of the Royal Ka," *JNES* 44 (1985): 251–94.

———. "The New Kingdom «Divine» Temple: the Example of Luxor," in B.E. Shafer, ed., *Temples of Ancient Egypt* (Ithaca, NY: Cornell University Press, 1997), pp. 127–84.

Bennett, Chris. "Queen Karimala, Daughter of Osochor?" *GM* 173 (1999): 7–8.

Bergman, Jan. *Isis-Seele und Osiris-Ei. Zwei ägyptologische Studien zu Diodorus Siculus I 27, 4–5,* Acta Universitatis Upsaliensis, Historia Religionem 4 (Uppsala and Stockholm: Almqvist and Wiksell, 1970).

Bernand, André. *La prose sur pierre dans l'Égypte hellénistique et romaine,* 2 vols. (Paris: Éditions du Centre National de la Recherche Scientifique, 1992).

Bickel, Susanne, Marc Gabolde, and Pierre Tallet. "Des annales héliopolitaines de la Troisième Période Intermédiaire," *BIFAO* 98 (1998): 31–56.

Blottière, Alain. *Vintage Egypt: Cruising the Nile in the Golden Age of Travel* (Paris: Éditions Flammarion, 2003).

Borghouts, Joris F. *The Magical Texts of Papyrus Leiden I 348,* OMRO 51 (Leiden: Brill, 1971).
———. "A Deputy of the Gang Knows his Business," in R.J. Demarée and J.J. Janssen, eds., *Gleanings from Deir el-Medîna,* Egyptologische Uitgaven I (Leiden: Nederlands Instituut voor het Nabije Oosten, 1982), pp. 71–99.
———. "On Certain Uses of the of the Stative," *Lingua Aegyptia* 9 (2001): 11-35.

Brack, Annelies, and Artur Brack. *Das Grab des Haremheb, Theben Nr. 78,* AV 35 (Mainz: Philipp von Zabern, 1980).

Brashear, W., and A. Bülow. *Magica Varia,* Papyrologica Bruxellensia 25 (Brussels: Fondation Égyptologique Reine Élisabeth, 1991).

Breyer, Francis. *Tanutamani: die Traumstele und ihr Umfeld,* ÄAT 57 (Wiesbaden: Harrassowitz, 2003).

Brunner, Helmut. "Mitanni in einem ägyptischen Text vor oder um 1500," *MIO* 4 (1956): 323–27.

Burckhardt, John Lewis. *Travels in Nubia* (London: John Murray, 1819).

Cailliaud, Frédéric. *Voyage à Méroé, au Fleuve Blanc, au dela de Fazozl dans le midi du royaume de Sennar, à Syouah et dans cinq autres oasis; fait dans les années 1819, 1820, 1821 et 1822* (Paris: Imprimerie de Rignoux, 1823).

Caminos, Ricardo A. *Late-Egyptian Miscellanies,* Brown Egyptological Studies 1 (London: Oxford University Press, 1954).
———. *The Chronicle of Prince Osorkon,* Analecta Orientalia 37 (Rome: Pontifical Biblical Institute, 1958).
———. "Papyrus Berlin 10463," *JEA* 49 (1963): 29–37.
———. "The Nitocris Adoption Stela," *JEA* 50 (1964): 71–101.
———. *The New-Kingdom Temples of Buhen,* 2 vols., ASE 33 (London: Egypt Exploration Society, 1974).
———. "The Recording of Inscriptions and Scenes in Tombs and Temples," in R.A. Caminos and H.G. Fischer, *Ancient Egyptian Epigraphy and Palaeography* (New York: Metropolitan Museum of Art, 1975).
———. *A Tale of Woe from a Hieratic Papyrus in the A.S. Pushkin Museum of Fine Arts in Moscow* (Oxford: Griffith Institute, Ashmolean Museum: 1977).
———. *Semna-Kumma* I: *The Temple of Semna,* ASE 37 (London: Egypt Exploration Society, 1998).
———. *Semna-Kumma* II: *The Temple of Kumma,* ASE 37 (London: Egypt Exploration Society, 1998).
———. "Notes on Queen Katimala's Inscribed Panel in the Temple of Semna," in C. Berger, G. Clerc, and N. Grimal, eds., *Hommages à Jean Leclant 2: Nubie, Soudan, Éthiopie,* BdÉ 106/2 (Cairo: Institut Français d'Archéologie Orientale, 1994), pp. 73–80.

Capel, Anne K. "Head of Queen Tiye," in A.K. Capel and G.E. Markoe, eds., *Mistress of the House, Mistress of Heaven: Women in Ancient Egypt* (New York: Hudson Hills, 1996), pp. 111–12 and 202 (catalogue no. 44).

Carnarvon, Earl of, and Howard Carter, with Francis Llewellyn Griffith, George Legrain, Georg Möller, Percy E. Newberry, and Wilhelm Spiegelberg. *Five Years' Explorations at Thebes, a Record of Work Done 1907–1911* (London, New York, Toronto, and Melbourne: Oxford University Press, 1912).

Casson, Lionel. *Ships and Seamanship in the Ancient World* (Princeton: Princeton University Press, 1973).

Cassonnet, P. *Études de néo-égyptien: Les temps seconds* i-sd̲m.f *et* i-iri.f sd̲m, *entre syntaxe et sémantique* (Paris: Cybèle, 2000).

Castiglioni, Alfredo, Angelo Castiglioni, and Jean Vercoutter. *Das Goldland der Pharaonen: die Entdeckung von Berenike Pancrisia* (Mainz: Philipp von Zabern, 1998).

Černý, Jaroslav. "Papyrus Salt 124 (Brit. Mus. 10055)," *JEA* 15 (1929): 243–58.

———. "The Abnormal-Hieratic Tablet Leiden I 431," in *Studies in Honor of Francis Llewellyn Griffith* (London: Egypt Exploration Society, 1932), pp. 46–56.

———. *Late Ramesside Letters,* Bibliotheca Aegyptiaca 9 (Brussels: Fondation Égyptologique Reine Élisabeth, 1939).

———. *Coptic Etymological Dictionary* (Cambridge: Cambridge University Press, 1976).

Černý, Jaroslav, and Alan H. Gardiner. *Hieratic Ostraca* 1 (Oxford: Oxford University Press, 1957).

Černý, Jaroslav, and Sarah I. Groll. *A Late Egyptian Grammar,* 3rd ed. (Rome: Pontifical Biblical Institute, 1984).

Chapman, Suzanne E., and Dows Dunham. *Decorated Chapels of the Meroitic Pyramids at Meroë and Barkal,* The Royal Cemeteries of Kush 3 (Boston: Museum of Fine Arts, 1952).

Clère, J.J. Review of Caminos and James, *Gebel Silsila I,* in *RdÉ* 17 (1965): 203–8.

———. "Un mot pour «mariage» en Égyptien de l'époque ramesside," *RdÉ* 20 (1968): 171–75.

Colin, F., and Françoise Labrique. "*Semenekh oudjat* à Baḥariya," in F. Labrique, ed., *Religions méditerranéennes et orientales de l'antiquité,* BdÉ 135 (Cairo: Institut Français d'Archéologie Orientale, 2002), pp. 45–78.

Colvile, H.E. *History of the Sudan Campaign,* Victorian War Series 4 (Nashville: The Battery Press, 1996 [reprint of 1889 edition]).

Cowdrey, H.E.J. "Christianity and the Morality of Warfare during the First Century of Crusading," in M. Bull and N. Housley, eds., *The Experience of Crusading* 1. *Western Approaches* (Cambridge: Cambridge University Press), pp. 175–92.

Crum, Walter Ewing. *A Coptic Dictionary* (Oxford: Oxford University Press, 1939).

Crum, Walter Ewing, and H.G. Evelyn White. *The Monastery of Epiphanius at Thebes. Part II: Coptic Ostraca and Papyri, Greek Ostraca and Papyri* (New York: Metropolitan Museum of Art, 1936).

Curryer, Betty Nelson. *Anchors: An Illustrated History* (Annapolis: Naval Institute Press, 1999).

Darnell, John Coleman. "Two Sieges in the Aethiopic Stelae," in Daniela Mendel and Ulrike Claudi, eds., *Ägypten im afro-orientalischen Kontext,* AAP Sondernummer (Cologne: Universität zu Köln, 1992), pp. 73–93.

———. "The Apotropaic Goddess in the Eye," *SAK* 24 (1997): 35–48.

———. "The Rock Inscriptions of Tjehemau at Abisko," *ZÄS* 130 (2003): 31–48.

Darnell, John Coleman. "Opening the Narrow Doors of the Desert: Discoveries of the Theban Desert Road Survey," in Renée Friedman, ed., *Egypt and Nubia—Gifts of the Desert* (London: British Museum Press, 2002), pp. 132–55.

Darnell, John Coleman, and Richard Jasnow. "On the Moabite Inscriptions of Ramesses II at Luxor Temple," *JNES* 52 (1993): 263–74.

Darnell, John Coleman, with contributions by Deborah Darnell, Renée Friedman, and Stan Hendrickx. *Theban Desert Road Survey in the Egyptian Western Desert 1: Gebel Tjauti Rock Inscriptions 1–45, and Wadi el-Ḥôl Rock Inscriptions 1–45*, OIP 119 (Chicago: The Oriental Institute of the University of Chicago, 2002).

Davies, W. Vivian. "New Fieldwork at Kurgus, the Pharaonic Inscriptions," *Sudan and Nubia* 2 (1998): 26–30.

———. "Kurgus 2000: the Egyptian Inscriptions," *Sudan and Nubia* 5 (2001): 46–58.

———. "Kurgus 2002: the Inscriptions and Rock-Drawings," *Sudan and Nubia* 7 (2003): 52–54.

———. "La frontière méridionale de l'empire: les égyptiens à Kurgus," *BSFE* 157 (2003): 23–37.

Deines, H. von, and Wolfhart Westendorf. *Wörterbuch der medizinischen Texte, erste Hälfte (ꜣ-r)*, Grundriss der Medizin der Alten Ägypter 8 (Berlin: Akademie-Verlag, 1961).

Depuyt, Leo. "Analyzing the Use of Idioms Past (with Special Focus on Sovereign Nubia)," *SAK* 27 (1999): 38–44.

Derchain, Philippe. *Le sacrifice de l'oryx*, Rites Égyptiens 1 (Brussels: Fondation Égyptologique Reine Élisabeth, 1962).

———. *Les Monuments religieux à l'entrée de l'Ouady Helal*, Elkab 1 (Brussels: Fondation Égyptologique Reine Élisabeth, 1971).

De Simone, Maria Costanza. "The 'C-Groups' Culture of Lower Nubia," in Barbara E. Barich and Maria C. Gatto, eds., *Dynamics of Populations, Movements and Responses to Climatic Change in Africa*, Proceedings of the First Workshop of the Forum for African Archaeology and Cultural Heritage (Rome: Bonsignori, 1997), pp. 112–24.

Donker Van Heel, K., and B.J.J. Haring, *Writing in a Workmen's Village. Scribal Practice in Ramesside Deir El-Medina*, Egyptologische Uitgaven 16 (Leiden: Nederlands Instituut voor het Nabije Oosten, 2003).

Drenkhahn, Rosemarie. *Die Elephantine-Stele des Sethnacht und ihr historischer Hintergrund*, Ägyptologische Abhandlungen 36 (Wiesbaden: Harrassowitz, 1980).

Edel, Elmar. "Notizen zu Fremdnamen in ägyptischen Quellen," *Or.* 40 (1971): 1–10.

Edgerton, William F., and John A. Wilson. *Historical Records of Ramses III*, SAOC 12 (Chicago: University of Chicago Press, 1936).

Edwards, David N. "Meroitic Settlement Archaeology," in Derek A. Welsby, ed., *Recent Research in Kushite History and Archaeology: Proceedings of the 8th International Conference for Meroitic Studies*, British Museum Occasional Paper No. 131 (London: British Museum Press, 1999), pp. 65–110.

Edwards, David N. *The Nubian Past: An Archaeology of the Sudan* (London and New York: Routledge, 2004).

Edwards, Iorwerth E.S. *Oracular Amuletic Decrees of the Late New Kingdom,* 2 vols., Hieratic Papyri in the British Museum, Fourth Series (London: British Museum Press, 1960).

Eide, Tormod, Tomas Hägg, Richard Holton Pierce, and László Török. *Fontes Historiae Nubiorum. Textual Sources for the History of the Middle Nile Region between the Eighth Century BC and the Sixth Century AD.* Vol. 1: *From the Eighth to the Mid-Fifth Century BC* (Bergen: University of Bergen, Department of Classics, 1994).

———. *Fontes Historiae Nubiorum. Textual Sources for the History of the Middle Nile Region between the Eighth Century BC and the Sixth Century AD.* Vol. 2: *From the Mid-Fifth to the First Century BC* (Bergen: University of Bergen, Department of Classics, 1996).

Eingartner, J. *Isis und ihre Dienerinnen in der Kunst der römischen Kaiserzeit,* Mnemosyne, Bibliotheca Classica Batava, Supplementum 115 (Leiden: Brill, 1991).

El-Aguizy, Ola. *A Palaeographical Study of Demotic Papyri,* MIFAO 113 (Cairo: Institut Français d'Archéologie Orientale, 1998).

El-Enany, Khaled. "Le «dieu» nubien Sésostris III," *BIFAO* 104/1 (2004): 207–13.

Epigraphic Survey. *Medinet Habu 1: Earlier Historical Records of Ramses III,* OIP 8 (Chicago: University of Chicago Press, 1930).

———. *Medinet Habu 2: Later Historical Records of Ramses III,* OIP 9 (Chicago: University of Chicago Press, 1932).

———. *Reliefs and Inscriptions at Karnak 3: The Bubastite Portal,* OIP 74 (Chicago: University of Chicago Press, 1954).

———. *Medinet Habu 8: The Eastern High Gate, with Translations of Texts,* OIP 94 (Chicago: University of Chicago Press, 1970).

———. *The Temple of Khonsu* 1: *Scenes of King Herihor in the Court,* OIP 100 (Chicago: The Oriental Institute of the University of Chicago, 1979).

———. *The Temple of Khonsu* 2: *Scenes and Inscriptions in the Court and the First Hypostyle Hall,* OIP 103 (Chicago: The Oriental Institute of the University of Chicago, 1981).

———. *Reliefs and Inscriptions at Luxor Temple* 1: *The Festival Procession of Opet in the Colonnade Hall,* OIP 112 (Chicago: The Oriental Institute of the University of Chicago, 1994).

———. *Reliefs and Inscriptions at Luxor Temple* 2: *The Façade, Portals, Upper Register Scenes, Columns, Marginalia, and Statuary in the Colonnade Hall,* OIP 116 (Chicago: The Oriental Institute of the University of Chicago, 1998).

Erichsen, Wolja. " hinter dem Namen des Verstorbenen," *Acta Orientalia* 6 (1928): 270–78.

———. *Demotisches Glossar* (Copenhagen: Ejnar Munksgaard, 1954).

Erman, Adolf. *Neuaegyptische Grammatik,* 2nd ed. (Leipzig: Wilhelm Engelmann, 1933).

Erman, Adolf, and Hermann Grapow, eds. *Wörterbuch der ägyptischen Sprache,* 5 vols., with *Belegstellen* in 5 vols., 6 parts, 4th ed. (Berlin: Akademie-Verlag, 1982).

Eyre, Christopher J. "The Semna Stelae: Quotation, Genre, and Functions of Literature," in S. Israelit-Groll, ed., *Studies in Egyptology Presented to Miriam Lichtheim* Vol. 1 (Jerusalem: Magnes Press and Hebrew University, 1990), pp. 134-65.

Fairman, H.W. "Two Ptolemaic Alphabetic Values of 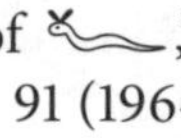," *JEA* 36 (1950): 110–11.

———. "Some Unrecorded Ptolemaic Words," *ZÄS* 91 (1964): 4–11.

Faulkner, Raymond O. *A Concise Dictionary of Middle Egyptian* (Oxford: Griffith Institute, 1976).

Fecht, Gerhard. *Wortakzent und Silbenstruktur. Untersuchungen zur Geschichte der ägyptischen Sprache,* Ägyptologische Forschungen 21 (Glückstadt, 1960).

Felber, Heinz. "Die demotische Chronik," in A. Blasius and B.U. Schipper, eds., *Apokalyptik und Ägypten, eine kritische Analyse der relevanten Texte aus dem griechisch-römischen Ägypten,* OLA 107 (Leuven: Peeters, 2002), pp. 65–111.

Feucht, Erika. *Das Grab des Nefersecheru (TT 296),* Theben 2 (Mainz: Philipp von Zabern, 1985).

Fischer, Henry G. "The Evolution of Composite Hieroglyphs in Ancient Egypt," *MMJ* 12 (1978): 5–19.

Fischer-Elfert, Hans-Werner. *Die satirische Streitschrift des Papyrus Anastasi I. Übersetzung und Kommentar,* Ägyptologische Abhandlungen 44 (Wiesbaden: Harrassowitz, 1986).

———. *Die satirische Streitschrift des Papyrus Anastasi I. Textzusammenstellung,* 2nd ed., Kleine Ägyptische Text (Wiesbaden: Harrassowitz, 1992).

———. "Viehdiebstahl im Ramessidischen Hermopolis," *Annals of the Naprstek Museum* 24 (2003): 73–87.

Frankfurter, David. *Elijah in Upper Egypt: The Apocalypse of Elijah and Early Egyptian Christianity,* Studies in Antiquity and Christianity (Minneapolis: Fortress, 1993).

Gabolde, Marc, Geneviève Galliano, et al. *Coptos, l'Égypte antique aux portes du désert* (Paris: Réunion des Musées Nationaux, 2000).

Gardiner, Alan H. *The Inscription of Mes, a Contribution to the Study of Egyptian Judicial Procedure,* UGÄA 4 (Leipzig: Hinrichs, 1905), pp. 89–140.

———. "Four Papyri of the 18th Dynasty from Kahun," *ZÄS* 43 (1906): 27–47.

———. *The Admonitions of an Egyptian Sage, from a Hieratic Papyrus in Leiden (Pap. Leiden 344 recto)* (Leipzig: Hinrichs, 1909).

———. *Notes on the Story of Sinuhe* (Paris: Librairie Honoré Champion Éditeur, 1916).

———. *Late-Egyptian Stories,* Bibliotheca Aegyptiaca 1 (Brussels: Fondation Égyptologique Reine Élisabeth, 1932).

———. *Late-Egyptian Miscellanies,* Bibliotheca Aegyptiaca 7 (Brussels: Fondation Égyptologique Reine Élisabeth, 1937).

———. "Ramesside Texts Relating to the Taxation and Transport of Corn," *JEA* 27 (1941): 19–73.

———. *Ramesside Administrative Documents* (Oxford: Griffith Institute, 1948).

———. "A Protest against Unjustified Tax-Demands," *RdÉ* 6 (1951): 115–33.

Gasse, Annie. *Données nouvelles administratives et sacerdotales sur l'organisation du domaine d'Amon, XXe–XXIe dynasties, à la lumière des papyrus Prachov, Reinhardt et Grundbuch (avec edition princeps des papyrus Louvre AF 6345 et 6346–7)* 2 vols., BdÉ 104 (Cairo: Institut Français d'Archéologie Orientale, 1988).

Germond, P. *Sekhmet et la protection du monde,* AH 9 (Geneva: Éditions de Belles-Lettres, 1981).

Gessler-Löhr, B. "Zur Schreibung von *mꜣꜥ-ḫrw* mit der Blume," *GM* 116 (1990): 25–43.

Gleichen, Count, ed. *The Anglo-Egyptian Sudan: a Compendium Prepared by Officers of the Sudan Government,* 2 vols. (London: Harrison and Sons, 1905).

Goebs, Katja. "*ḫftj nṯr* as Euphemism—the Case of the Antef Decree," *JEA* 89 (2003): 27–37.

Goldwasser, Orly. "On the Choice of Registers—Studies on the Grammar of Papyrus Anastasi I," in Sarah Israelit-Groll, ed., *Studies in Egyptology Presented to Miriam Lichtheim* 1 (Jerusalem: Magnes Press, 1990), pp. 200–40.

Goyon, Jean-Claude. "Sur une formule des rituels de conjuration des dangers de l'année," *BIFAO* 74 (1974): 77–83.

———. *Le Papyrus d'Imouthès fils de Psintaês* (New York: Metropolitan Museum of Art, 1999).

Grandet, P. *Le Papyrus Harris I,* 3 vols. BdÉ 109 (Cairo: Institut Français d'Archéologie Orientale, 1994).

Grapow, Hermann. *Die bildlichen Ausdrücke des Ägyptischen. Vom Denken und Dichten einer altorientalischen Sprache* (Leipzig: Hinrichs, 1924).

———. "Die Inschrift der Königin Katimala am Tempel von Semne," *ZÄS* 76 (1940): 24–41.

Green, M.A. "The Passing of Harmose," *Orientalia* 45 (1976): 395–409.

Grimal, Nicolas-Christophe. *La stèle triomphale de Pi(ꜥankhi) au Musée du Caire, JE 48862 et 47086–47089,* Études sur la propagande royale égyptienne 1, MIFAO 105 (Cairo: Institut Français d'Archéologie Orientale, 1981).

———. *Quatre stèles napatéennes au Musée du Caire, JE 48863–48866, textes et indices,* Études sur la propagande royale égyptienne 2, MIFAO 106 (Cairo: Institut Français d'Archéologie Orientale, 1981).

———. *Les termes de la propagande royale égyptienne, de la XIXe dynastie à la conquête d'Alexandre,* Institut de France, Mémoires de l'Academie des Inscriptions et Belles-Lettres, Nouvelle Série tome 6 (Paris: Imprimerie Nationale, 1986).

Groll, Sarah I. *Non-Verbal Sentence Patterns in Late Egyptian* (London: Oxford University Press, 1967).

Habachi, Labib. *The Second Stela of Kamose and his Struggle against the Hyksos Ruler and his Capital,* ADAIK 8 (Glückstadt: Augustin, 1972).

———. "Königssohn von Kusch," in W. Helck and W. Westendorf, eds., *Lexikon der Ägyptologie* 3 (Wiesbaden: Harrassowitz, 1979): cols. 630–40.

Hannig, Rainer. *Ägyptisches Wörterbuch I, Altes Reich und Erste Zwischenzeit,* Hannig-Lexica 4 (Mainz: Philipp von Zabern, 2003).

Haring, B.J.J. *Divine Households: Administrative and Economic Aspects of the New Kingdom Royal Memorial Temples in Western Thebes,* Egyptologische Uitgaven 12 (Leiden: Nederlands Instituut voor het Nabije Oosten, 1997).

Harrell, James A. "Pharaonic Stone Quarries in the Egyptian Deserts," in Renée Friedman, ed., *Egypt and Nubia—Gifts of the Desert* (London: British Museum Press, 2002), pp. 232–43.

Heidorn, Lisa. *The Fortress of Dorginarti and Lower Nubia during the Seventh to Fifth Centuries* B.C. (unpublished Ph.D. dissertation, University of Chicago, 1992).

———. "Historical Implications of the Pottery from the Earliest Tombs at El-Kurru," *JARCE* 31 (1994): 115–31.

Helck, Wolfgang. *Urkunden der 18. Dynastie, Heft 22: Inschriften der Könige von Amenophis III. bis Haremheb und ihrer Zeitgenossen* (Berlin: Akademie-Verlag, 1958).

———. *Historisch-biographische Texte der 2. Zwischenzeit und neue Texte der 18. Dynastie,* KÄT 5, 3rd ed. (Wiesbaden: Harrassowitz, 2002).

———. *Die Prophezeiung des Nfr.tj,* 2nd ed., KÄT (Wiesbaden: Harrassowitz, 1992).

Helck, Wolfgang, and Wolfhart Westendorf, eds., *Lexikon der Ägyptologie,* 7 vols. (Wiesbaden: Harrassowitz, 1975–1992).

Hinkel, Friedrich W. *Exodus from Nubia* (Berlin: Akademie-Verlag, 1978).

Hintze, Fritz. *Untersuchungen zu Stil und Sprache neuägyptischer Erzählungen,* Vol. 1, Deutsche Akademie der Wissenschaften zu Berlin, Institut für Orientforschung, Veröffentlichung 2 (Berlin: Akademie-Verlag, 1950).

Hoffmann, Friedhelm. *Ägypten: Kultur und Lebenswelt in griechisch-römischer Zeit, eine Darstellung nach den demotischen Quellen* (Berlin: Akademie-Verlag, 2000).

Hofmann, Beate. *Die Königsnovelle: "Strukturanalyse am Einzelwerk",* ÄAT 62 (Wiesbaden: Harrassowitz, 2004).

Hofmann, Inge. "Die ältesten Belege für das Meroitische anhand von Personennamen," *SUGIA—Sprache und Geschichte in Afrika* 3 (1981): 7–15.

———. "Die meroitische Religion. Staatskult und Volksfrömmigkeit," in W. Haase and H. Temporini, eds., *Aufstieg und Niedergang der römischen Welt* Teil II: *Principat*, Band 18: *Religion,* 5. Teilband: *Heidentum: die religiösen Verhältnisse in den Provinzen (Forts.)* (Berlin and New York: Walter de Gruyter, 1995), pp. 2801–68.

———. "Zur Herkunft der meroitischen Spiegeltypen," in Hartwig Altenmüller and Renate Germer, eds., *Miscellanea Aegyptologica, Wolfgang Helck zum 75. Geburtstag* (Hamburg: Archäologisches Institut der Universität Hamburg, 1989), pp. 97–118.

Horden, Peregrine, and Nicholas Purcell. *The Corrupting Sea: a Study of Mediterranean History* (Oxford: Blackwell, 2004).

Horne, Lee. "Occupational and locational instability in arid land settlement," in Catherine M. Cameron and Steve A. Tomka, eds., *Abandonment of settlements and regions. Ethnoarchaeological and archaeological approaches* (Cambridge: Cambridge University Press, 1993), pp. 43–53.

Hourani, George F. *Arab Seafaring,* expanded edition, revised by John Carswell (Princeton: Princeton University Press, 1995).

Hull, Richard W. *African Cities and Towns before the European Conquest* (New York and London: W.W. Norton, 1976).

Hume, W.F. *Geology of Egypt 2: The Fundamental Pre-Cambrian Rocks of Egypt and the Sudan; their Distribution, Age, and Character* Part 1: *The Metamorphic Rocks,* Survey of Egypt (Cairo: Government Press, 1934).

Husson, Constance. *L'offrande du miroir dans les temples égyptiens de l'époque gréco-romaine* (Lyon: Audin, 1977).

Jacquet-Gordon, Helen. Review of I.E.S. Edwards, *Oracular Amuletic Decrees,* in *Bi.Or.* 20 (1963): 31–33.

Jansen-Winkeln, Karl. *Ägyptische Biographien der 22. und 23. Dynastie,* 2 vols., ÄAT 8 (Wiesbaden: Harrassowitz, 1985).
———. "Das Ende des Neuen Reiches," *ZÄS* 119 (1992): 22–37.
———. "Die ägyptische 'Könignovelle' als Texttyp," *WZKM* 83 (1993): 101–16.
———. "Der Beginn der libyschen Herrschaft in Ägypten," *BN* 71 (1994): 78–97.
———. *Text und Sprache in der 3. Zwischenzeit. Vorarbeiten zu einer spätmittelägyptischen Grammatik,* ÄAT 26 (Wiesbaden: Harrassowitz, 1994).
———. "Diglossie und Zweisprachigkeit," *WZKM* 85 (1995): 92–102.
———. "Die Plünderung der Königsgräber des Neuen Reiches," *ZÄS* 122 (1995): 62–78.
———. *Spätmittelägyptische Grammatik der Texte der 3. Zwischenzeit,* ÄAT 34 (Wiesbaden: Harrassowitz, 1996).
———. *Sentenzen und Maximen in den Privatinschriften der ägyptischen Spätzeit,* Achet B1 (Berlin: Achet, 1999).

Janssen, Jac J. *Commodity Prices from the Ramessid Period, an Economic Study of the Village of Necropolis Workmen at Thebes* (Leiden: Brill, 1975).

Jasnow, Richard. *A Late Period Hieratic Wisdom Text (P. Brooklyn 47.218.135),* SAOC 52 (Chicago: The Oriental Institute of the University of Chicago, 1992).
———. "Remarks on Continuity in Egyptian Literary Tradition," in E. Teeter and J.A. Larson, eds., *Gold of Praise, Studies on Ancient Egypt in Honor of Edward F. Wente,* SAOC 58 (Chicago: The Oriental Institute of the University of Chicago, 1999), pp. 193–210.
———. "Egypt, Middle Kingdom and Second Intermediate Period," in R. Westbrook, ed., *A History of Ancient Near Eastern Law,* Handbuch der Orientalistik I/72/1 (Leiden: Brill, 2003), pp. 255–88.

Jeffreys, D.G., and Jaromir Malek. "Memphis 1986, 1987," *JEA* 74 (1988): 15–29.

Johnson, Janet H. *The Demotic Verbal System,* SAOC 38 (Chicago: The Oriental Institute of the University of Chicago, 1976).
———. "The Demotic Chronicle as a Statement of a Theory of Kingship," *JSSEA* 13 (1983): 61–72.

Junge, Friedrich, trans. David Warburton. *Late Egyptian Grammar: An Introduction* (Oxford: Griffith Institute, 2001).

Junker, Hermann "Die Feinde auf dem Sockel der Chasechem-Statuen und die Darstellung von geopferten Tieren," in Otto Firchow, ed., *Ägyptologische Studien,* Deutsche Akademie der Wissenschaften zu Berlin, Institut für Orientforschung, Veröffentlichung 29 (Berlin: 1955), pp. 162–74.

Kadish, Gerald E. "British Museum Writing Board 5645: The Complaints of Kha-kheper-Rēʿ-senebu," *JEA* 59 (1973): 77–90.

Kees, Hermann. *Das Priestertum im ägyptischen Staat vom Neuen Reich bis zur Spätzeit,* Probleme der Ägyptologie 1 (Leiden: Brill, 1953).

Kemp, Barry J. *Ancient Egypt: Anatomy of a Civilization* (London and New York: Routledge, 1995 [reprint of 1989 edition]).

Kendall, Timothy. "The Origin of the Napatan State: El Kurru and the Evidence for the Royal Ancestors," in S. Wenig, ed., *Studien zum antiken Sudan: Akten der 7. Internationalen Tagung für meroitische Forschungen,* Meroitica 15 (Wiesbaden: Harrassowitz, 1999), pp. 3–117.

———. "A Response to László Török's 'Long Chronology' of El Kurru," in S. Wenig, ed., *Studien zum antiken Sudan: Akten der 7. Internationalen Tagung für meroitische Forschungen,* Meroitica 15 (Wiesbaden: Harrassowitz, 1999), pp. 164–76.

Kitchen, Kenneth A. *The Third Intermediate Period in Egypt (1100–650 B.C.),* 2nd rev. ed. (Warminster: Aris and Phillips, 1986).

———. *Ramesside Inscriptions 2: Historical and Biographical* (Oxford: Blackwell, 1979).

———. *Ramesside Inscriptions. Translated and Annotated, Notes and Comments* 2 (Oxford: Blackwell, 1999).

Klemm, Dietrich D., and Rosemarie Klemm. "Antiker Goldbergbau in der ägyptisch-sudanesischen Ostwüste," *Nürnberger Blätter zur Archäologie* 13 (1997): 149–66.

———. "Chronologischer Abriss der antiken Goldgewinnung in der Ostwüste Ägyptens," *MDAIK* 50 (1994): 189–222.

Klemm, Dietrich D., Rosemarie Klemm, and Andreas Murr, "Ancient Gold Mining in the Eastern Desert of Egypt and the Nubian Desert of Sudan," in Renée Friedman, ed., *Egypt and Nubia—Gifts of the Desert* (London: British Museum Press, 2002), pp. 215–31.

Koch, Roland. *Die Erzählung des Sinuhe,* Bibliotheca Aegyptiaca 17 (Brussels: Fondation Égyptologique Reine Élisabeth, 1990).

Koenig, Yvan. *Le papyrus Boulaq 6,* BdÉ 87 (Cairo: Institut Français d'Archéologie Orientale, 1981).

Kormysheva, Éléonore. "Le nom d'Amon sur les monuments royaux de Kouch, études lexicographiques," in C. Berger, G. Clerc, and N. Grimal, eds., *Hommages à Jean Leclant 2: Nubie, Soudan, Éthiopie,* BdÉ 106/2 (Cairo: Institut Français d'Archéologie Orientale, 1994), pp. 251–61.

Kruchten, Jean-Marie. *Études de syntaxe néo-égyptienne,* Annuaire de l'Institut de Philologie et d'Histoire Orientales et Slaves, Supplément 1 (Brussels: Éditions de l'Université de Bruxelles, 1982).

———. *Le grand texte oraculaire de Djéhoutymose, intendant du domaine d'Amon sous le pontificat de Pinedjem II,* Monographies Reine Élisabeth 5 (Brussels: Fondation Égyptologique Reine Élisabeth, 1986).

———. *Les annales des prêtres de Karnak (XXI–XXIIIemes Dynasties) et autres textes contemporains relatifs à l'initiation des prêtres d'Amon,* Orientalia Lovaniensia Analecta 32 (Leuven: Peeters, 1989).

Layton, Bentley. *A Coptic Grammar,* Porta Linguarum Orientalium 20 (Wiesbaden: Harrassowitz, 2000).

Leclant, Jean. "Osiris *pꜣ-wšb-iꜣd,*" in O. Firchow, ed., *Ägyptologische Studien [Hermann Grapow zum 70. Geburtstag gewidmet],* Deutsche Akademie der

Wissenschaften zu Berlin, Institut für Orientforschung, Veröffentlichung 29 (Berlin: Akademie-Verlag, 1955), pp. 197–204.

Lefebvre, Gustave. *Inscriptions concernant les grands prêtres d'Amon Romê-Royÿ et Amenhotep* (Paris: Librairie Orientaliste Paul Geuthner, 1929).

Lesko, Leonard H., ed. *A Late Egyptian Dictionary* 1 (Berkeley: B.C. Scribe, 1982).

———. *A Late Egyptian Dictionary* 2 (Berkeley: B.C. Scribe, 1984).

Lichtheim, Miriam. *Ancient Egyptian Literature, a Book of Readings* 1 (Berkeley: University of California Press, 1973).

———. "The Stela of Taniy, CG 20564, its Date and its Character," *SAK* 16 (1989): 203–15.

Liverani, Irene. "Hillat El-Arab," in Derek A. Welsby and Julie R. Anderson, eds., *Sudan, Ancient Treasures: an Exhibition of Recent Discoveries from the Sudan National Museum* (London: British Museum Press, 2004), pp. 138–47.

Lohwasser, Angelika. *Die königlichen Frauen im antiken Reich von Kusch, 25. Dynastie bis zur Zeit des Nestasen,* Meroitica 19 (Wiesbaden: Harrassowitz, 2001).

———. "Der 'Thronschatz' der Königin Amanishakheto," in Caris-Beatrice Arnst, Ingelore Hafemann, and Angelika Lohwasser, eds., *Begegnungen: Antike Kulturen im Niltal* (Leipzig: Wodtke und Stegbauer, 2001), pp. 285–302.

Loprieno, Antonio. *Ancient Egyptian, a linguistic introduction* (Cambridge: Cambridge University Press, 1995).

———. "Views of the Past in Egypt during the First Millennium BC," in J. Tait, ed., *'Never Had the Like Occurred:' Egypt's View of its Past* (London: UCL / Institute of Archaeology, 2003), pp. 139–54.

Lustman, Jacqueline. *Étude grammaticale du papyrus Bremner-Rhind* (Paris: Mistral Photo, 1999).

Macadam, M.F. Laming. *The Temples of Kawa,* 2 vols. (London: Griffith Institute, 1949–1955).

Manassa, Colleen. *The Great Karnak Inscription of Merneptah: Grand Strategy in the 13th Century* BC, YES 5 (New Haven: Yale Egyptological Seminar, 2003).

Marciniak, Marek. "Quelques remarques sur la formule *ir nfr, ir nfr,*" *Études et travaux* 2, Travaux du Centre d'Archéologie Méditerranéenne de l'Académie Polonaise des Sciences 6 (Warsaw: Éditions Scientifiques de Pologne, 1968), pp. 25–31.

———. *Les inscriptions hiératiques du temple de Thoutmosis III,* Deir el-Bahari 1 (Warsaw: Éditions Scientifiques de Pologne, 1974).

McDowell, Andrea G. *Jurisdiction in the Workmen's Community of Deir El-Medîna,* Egyptologische Uitgaven 5 (Leiden: Nederlands Instituut voor het Nabije Oosten, 1990).

Meeks, Dimitri. *Année lexicographique,* 3 vols. (Paris: D. Meeks, 1980–1982).

Meyer-Dietrich, E. *Nechet und Nil, ein ägyptischer Frauensarg des Mittleren Reiches aus religionsökologischer Sicht,* Acta Universitatis Upsaliensis, Historia Religionum 18 (Uppsala: Uppsala University Press, 2001).

Möller, Georg. *Hieratische Paläographie, Die ägyptische Buchschrift in ihrer Entwicklung von der fünften Dynastie bis zur Römischen Kaiserzeit,* 3 vols., 2nd revised edition (Leipzig: Hinrichs, 1927).

Morkot, Robert. "The Foundations of the Kushite State. A Response to the Paper of László Török," *CRIPEL* 17/1 (1995): 229–42.

———. "Kingship and Kinship in the Empire of Kush," in S. Wenig, ed., *Studien zum antiken Sudan: Akten der 7. Internationalen Tagung für meroitische Forschungen,* Meroitica 15 (Wiesbaden: Harrassowitz, 1999), pp. 179–229.

———. "The Origin of the 'Napatan' State," in S. Wenig, ed., *Studien zum antiken Sudan: Akten der 7. Internationalen Tagung für meroitische Forschungen,* Meroitica 15 (Wiesbaden: Harrassowitz, 1999), pp. 139–48.

Morschauser, Scott. "Observations on the Speeches of Ramesses II in the Literary Record of the Battle of Kadesh," in H. Goedicke, ed., *Perspectives on the Battle of Kadesh* (Baltimore: Halgo, 1985), pp. 123–206.

Müller, Christa. "Spiegel," *LdÄ* 5 (1984): cols. 1147–50.

Müller, W. Max. *Egyptological Researches, Results of a Journey in 1906,* 2, Carnegie Institution of Washington Publication No. 53, Volume II (Washington, DC: Gibson Brothers, 1910).

Müller-Winkler, C. *Die ägyptischen Objekt-Amulette,* OBO Series Archaeologica 5 (Göttingen: Vandenhoeck & Ruprecht, 1987).

Müller-Wollermann, Renate. *Vergehen und Strafen: Zur Sanktionierung abweichenden Verhaltens im alten Ägypten,* Probleme der Ägyptologie 21 (Leiden: Brill, 2004).

Münster, Maria. *Untersuchungen zur Göttin Isis, vom Alten Reich bis zum Ende des Neuen Reiches,* MÄS 11 (Berlin: Bruno Hessling, 1968).

Munro, Peter. "Eine Gruppe spätägyptischer Bronzespiegel," *ZÄS* 95 (1969): 92–109.

Murnane, William J., and Charles C. Van Siclen, *The Boundary Stelae of Akhenaton* (London and New York: Kegan Paul International, 1993).

Murray, G.W. *Sons of Ishmael, a Study of the Egyptian Bedouin* (London: Routledge, 1935).

Naguib, Saphinaz-Amal. *Le clergé féminin d'Amon thébain à la 21e Dynastie,* Orientalia Lovaniensa Analecta 38 (Leuven: Peeters, 1990).

Neveu, François. *La particule ḫr en néo-égyptien, étude synchronique,* Études et Mémoires d'Égyptologie 4 (Paris: Cybèle, 2001).

Niwiński, Andrzej. "Le passage de la XXe à la XXIIe dynastie: chronologie et histoire politique," *BIFAO* 95 (1995): 329–60,

Obsomer, Claude. *Sésostris Ier, étude chronologique et historique du règne* (Brussels: Connaissance de l'Égypte Ancienne, 1995).

O'Connor, David. "New Kingdom and Third Intermediate Period, 1552–664 BC," in B.G. Trigger, B.J. Kemp, D. O'Connor, and A.B. Lloyd, *Ancient Egypt, a Social History* (Cambridge: Cambridge University Press, 1983), pp. 183–278.

O'Connor, David, and David P. Silverman, eds., *Ancient Egyptian Kingship,* Probleme der Ägyptologie 9 (Leiden: Brill, 1995).

Osing, Jürgen. *Die Nominalbildung des Ägyptischen,* 2 vols. (Mainz: Philipp von Zabern, 1976).

Parkinson, Richard B. *Voices from Ancient Egypt, an Anthology of Middle Kingdom Writings* (London: British Museum Press, 1991).

———. *The Tale of Sinuhe and Other Ancient Egyptian Poems 1940–1640 BC* (Oxford: Oxford University Press, 1997).

———. "The Text of *Khakheperreseneb*: New Readings of EA 5645, and an Unpublished Ostracon," *JEA* 83 (1997): 55–68.

Paul, A. *A History of the Beja Tribes of the Sudan* (Cambridge: Cambridge University Press, 1954).

Peden, Alexander J. *The Graffiti of Pharaonic Egypt, Scope and Roles of Informal Writings (c. 3100–332 BC),* Probleme der Ägyptologie 17 (Leiden: Brill, 2001).

Peet, Thomas Eric. *Great Tomb Robberies of the Twentieth Egyptian Dynasty; being a critical study, with translations and commentaries, of the papyri in which these are recorded* (Oxford: Clarendon, 1930).

Perdu, Olivier. "Le Monument de Samtoutefnakht à Naples," *RdÉ* 36 (1985): 89–113.

———. "Florilège d'incitations à agir," *RdÉ* 51 (2000): 175–93.

Petrie, William Matthew Flinders, with D.G. Hogarth. *Koptos* (London: Bernard Quaritch, 1896).

Petrie, William Matthew Flinders. *Amulets, Illustrated by the Egyptian Collection in University College, London* (London: Constable, 1914).

Peust, Carsten. *Das Napatanische: Ein ägyptischer Dialekt aus dem Nubien des späten ersten vorchristlichen Jahrtausends,* Monographien zur ägyptischen Sprache 3 (Göttingen: Peust und Gutschmidt, 1999).

Piankoff, Alexandre, and Natasha Rambova, *Mythological Papyri,* 2 vols., Bollingen Series 40/3 (New York: Pantheon, 1957),

Piccione, Peter A. "Sportive Fencing as a Ritual for Destroying the Enemies of Horus," in E. Teeter and J. Larson, eds., *Gold of Praise,* SAOC 58 (Chicago: The Oriental Institute of the University of Chicago, 1999), pp. 335–49.

Piehl, K. "Deux inscriptions de Mendès," *Recueil de travaux* 3 (1882): 27–31.

Pomerantseva, Natalie. "The Canonical Structure of Some Meroitic Relief Compositions," in D.A. Welsby, ed., *Recent Research in Kushite History and Archaeology: Proceedings of the 8th International Conference for Meroitic Studies,* British Museum Occasional Paper 131 (London: British Museum Press, 1999), pp. 277–84.

Porten, Bezalel, ed. *The Elephantine Papyri in English* (Leiden: Brill, 1996).

Porter, Bertha, and Rosalind L.B. Moss. *Topographical Bibliography of Ancient Egyptian Hieroglyphic Texts, Reliefs and Paintings* 7: *Nubia, the Deserts, and Outside Egypt* (Oxford: Clarendon, 1952).

Porter, Bertha, Rosalind Moss, and E. Burney. *Topographical Bibliography of Ancient Egyptian Hieroglyphic Texts, Reliefs, and Paintings* 2: *Theban Temples,* 2nd ed. (Oxford: Clarendon, 1972).

Posener, Georges. *La première domination perse en Égypte, recueil d'inscriptions hiéroglyphiques,* BdÉ 11 (Cairo: Institut Français d'Archéologie Orientale, 1936).
———. *L'Enseignement loyaliste, sagesse égyptienne du Moyen Empire,* Centre de Recherches d'Histoire et de Philosophie de la IVe Section de l'École Pratique des Hautes Études II, Hautes Études Orientales 5 (Geneva: Librairie Droz, 1976).
———. *Cinq figurines d'envoûtement,* BdÉ 101 (Cairo: Institut Français d'Archéologie Orientale, 1987).

Priese, Karl-Heinz. "Der Beginn der der kuschitischen Herrschaft in Ägypten," *ZÄS* 98 (1972): 16–32.
———. "Zur Sprache der ägyptischen Inschriften der Könige von Kusch," *ZÄS* 98 (1972): 99–124.

Quaegebeur, Jan. "Reines ptolémaïques et traditions égyptiennes," in H. Maehler and V.M. Strocka, eds., *Das ptolemaïsche Ägypten, Akten des internationalen Symposions 27.–29. September 1976 in Berlin* (Mainz: Philipp von Zabern, 1978), pp. 245–62.

Quirke, Stephen. "Women in Ancient Egypt: Temple Titles and Funerary Papyri," in A. Leahy and J. Tait, eds., *Studies on Ancient Egypt in Honour of H.S. Smith,* Occasional Publications 13 (London: Egypt Exploration Society, 1999), pp., 227–35.

Ranke, Hermann. *Die ägyptischen Personennamen,* 2 vols. (Glückstadt: J.J. Augustin, 1935 and 1925).

Redford, Donald B. *Pharaonic King-Lists, Annals and Day-Books, a Contribution to the Study of the Egyptian Sense of History,* SSEA Publication 4 (Mississauga: Benben Publications, 1986).
———. *From Slave to Pharaoh: the Black Experience of Ancient Egypt* (Baltimore: Johns Hopkins University Press, 2004).

Reisner, George Andrew, Dows Dunham, and Jozef M.A. Janssen, *Semna Kumma,* Second Cataract Forts 1 (Boston: Museum of Fine Arts, 1960).

Reisner, M.B. "Inscribed Monuments from Gebel Barkal, Part 4. The Stela of Prince Khaliut," *ZÄS* 70 (1934): 34–46.

Ritner, Robert Kriech. *The Mechanics of Ancient Egyptian Magical Practice,* SAOC 54 (Chicago: The Oriental Institute of the University of Chicago, 1993).

Robson, Brian. *Fuzzy Wuzzy, the Campaigns in the Eastern Sudan, 1884–85* (Tunbridge Wells: Spellmount, 1993).

Rondot, Vincent. *La Grande salle hypostyle de Karnak: les architraves* (Paris: Éditions Recherche sur les Civilisations, 1997).

Rossi, F., and W. Pleyte. *Papyrus de Turin* (Leiden: Brill, 1869–1876).

Roth, Silke. *Gebieterin aller Länder: Die Rolle der königlichen Frauen in der fiktiven und realen Aussenpolitik des ägyptischen Neuen Reiches,* OBO 185 (Göttingen: Vandenhoeck & Ruprecht: 2002).

Russell Pasha, Thomas. *Egyptian Service, 1902–1946* (London: John Murray, 1949).

Sadr, Karim. *The Development of Nomadism in Ancient Northeast Africa* (Philadelphia: University of Pennsylvania Press, 1991).

Sargent, Cara Lia. *The Napatan Royal Inscriptions: Egyptian in Nubia* (unpublished Ph.D. dissertation, Yale University, 2004).

Sauneron, Serge. *Un traité d'ophiologie.* Bibliothèque Générale 11 (Cairo: Institut Français d'Archéologie Orientale, 1989).

Schade-Busch, Mechthild. *Zur Königsideologie Amenophis' III.*, HÄB 35 (Hildesheim: Gerstenberg, 1992).

Schulman, Alan R. "The Kushite Connection," in *Studies in Honor of William Kelly Simpson* 2 (Boston: Museum of Fine Arts, 1996), pp. 713–15.

Schwaller de Lubicz, R.A., with Georges and Valentine de Miré, and Lucie Lamy, translated by Jon Graham, *The Temples of Karnak* (Rochester: Inner Traditions International, 1999).

Seidlmayer, Stephan Johannes. "Epigraphische Bemerkungen zur Stele des Sethnachte aus Elephantine," in Heike Guksch and Daniel Polz, eds., *Stationen: Beiträge zur Kulturgeschichte Ägyptens Rainer Stadelmann gewidmet* (Mainz: Philipp von Zabern, 1998), pp. 363–86.

———. "Zu Fundort und Aufstellungskontext der großen Semna-Stele Sesostris' III.," *Studien zur altägyptischen Kultur* 28 (2000): 233–42.

Sethe, Kurt. *Das aegyptische Verbum im Altaegyptischen, Neuaegyptischen und Koptischen,* 3 vols. (Leipzig: Hinrichs, 1899–1902).

———. "ⲙⲛ̄ⲧϥ -ⲥⲱⲧⲙ̄ 'er kann nicht hören'," *ZÄS* 57 (1920): 138.

———. *Urkunden der 18. Dynastie* I: *Historisch-biographische Urkunden aus den Zeiten der Hyksosvertreiber und ihrer ersten Nachfolger,* 2nd ed. (Leipzig: Hinrichs, 1927).

———. *Übersetzung und Kommentar zu den altägyptischen Pyramidentexten* (Glückstadt: J.J. Augustin, 1935–62).

———. *Ägyptische Lesestücke zum Gebrauch im akademischen Unterricht: Texte des mittleren Reiches* (Leipzig: Hinrichs, 1928).

Siclen, Charles van. "Egyptian Antiquities in South Texas, Part 2. A Kohl Jar of Queen Mereseger," *VA* 8 (1992): 29–32.

Sieber-Lehmann, Claudius. "An Obscure but Powerful Pattern: Crusading, Nationalism and the Swiss Confederation in the Late Middle Ages," in Norman Housley, ed., *Crusading in the Fifteenth Century: Message and Impact* (New York: Macmillan Palgrave, 2004), pp. 81–93.

Silverman, David P. "An Emphasized Object of a Nominal Verb in Middle Egyptian," *Or* 49 (1980): 199–203.

Simpson, William Kelly. *Heka-Nefer and the Dynastic Material from Toshka and Arminna,* Publications of the Pennsylvania-Yale Expedition to Egypt 1 (New Haven: Peabody Museum, 1963).

Smith, Harry S. *The Fortress of Buhen,* Excavation Memoir 48 (London: Egypt Exploration Society, 1976).

Smith, Mark. "Sonnenauge, Demotischer Mythos vom," in W. Helck and W. Westendorf, eds., *Lexikon der Ägyptologie* 5 (Wiesbaden: Harrassowitz, 1984), cols. 1082–87.

Smith, Stuart Tyson. *Askut in Nubia: the Economics and Ideology of Egyptian Imperialism in the Second Millennium B.C.* (London and New York: Kegan Paul International, 1995).

Spalinger, Anthony J. *Aspects of the Military Documents of the Ancient Egyptians* (New Haven: Yale University Press, 1982).

Spiegelberg, Wilhelm. "Koptische Miscellen, §XII–XXI," *RdT* 26 (1904): 34–40.

———. *Demotische Grammatik* (Heidelberg: Carl Winters, 1925).

Steindorff, Georg. *Aniba* 2, Service des Antiquités de l'Égypte, Mission Archéologique de Nubie 1929–1934 (Glückstadt: J.J. Augustin, 1937).

Stern, Ludwig. *Koptische Grammatik* (reprint Osnabrück: Biblio, 1971),

Sweeney, Deborah. "Idiolects in the Late Ramesside Letters," *Lingua Aegyptia* 4 (1994): 275–324.

———. *Correspondence and Dialogue: Pragmatic Factors in Late Ramesside Letter-Writing,* ÄAT 49 (Wiesbaden: Harrassowitz, 2001).

te Velde, Herman. "Towards a Minimal Definition of the Goddess Mut," *JEOL* 26 (1979/80): 3–9.

te Velde, Herman. "Mut, the Eye of Re," in Silvia Shoske, ed., *Akten des vierten internationalen Ägyptologen-Kongresses, München 1985* 3 (Hamburg: H. Buske, 1988), pp. 395–403.

Thiry, Jacques. *Le Sahara libyen dans l'Afrique du nord medievale,* Orientalia Lovaniensa Analecta 72 (Leuven: Peeters, 1995).

Thissen, Heinz-Josef. "Das Lamm des Bokchoris," in in A. Blasius and B.U. Schipper, eds., *Apokalyptik und Ägypten, eine kritische Analyse der relevanten Texte aus dem griechisch-römischen Ägypten,* Orientalia Lovaniensa Analecta 107 (Leuven: Peeters, 2002), pp. 113–38.

Till, Walter C. *Koptische Grammatik (saïdischer Dialekt), mit Bibliographie, Lesestücken und Wörterverzeichnissen,* Lehrbücher für das Studium der Orientalischen und Afrikanischen Sprachen 1, 4th ed. (Leipzig: VEB Verlag Enzyklopädie, 1970).

Török, László. *The Royal Crowns of Kush: a Study in Middle Nile Valley Regalia and Iconography in the First Millennia BC and AD,* Cambridge Monographs in African Archaeology 18, BAR International Series 338 (Oxford: BAR, 1987).

———. *The Birth of an Ancient African Kingdom: Kush and her Myth of the State in the First Millenium*(sic) *BC,* CRIPEL Supplément 4 (Lille: Université Charles-de-Gaulle, 1995).

———. "The Emergence of the Kingdom of Kush and her Myth of the State in the First Millennium BC," *CRIPEL* 17/1 (1995): 203–28.

———. *The Kingdom of Kush: Handbook of the Napatan-Meroitic Civilization,* Handbuch der Orientalistik, 1. Abteilung, Bd. 31 (Leiden: Brill, 1997).

———. "The Origin of the Napatan State: the Long Chronology of the El Kurru Cemetery: a Contribution to T. Kendall's Main Paper," in S. Wenig, ed., *Studien zum antiken Sudan: Akten der 7. Internationalen Tagung für meroitische Forschungen,* Meroitica 15 (Wiesbaden: Harrassowitz, 1999), pp. 149–59.

———. "On the Foundations of Kingship Ideology in the Empire of Kush," in S. Wenig, ed., *Studien zum antiken Sudan: Akten der 7. Internationalen Tagung für meroitische Forschungen,* Meroitica 15 (Wiesbaden: Harrassowitz, 1999), pp. 273–87.

Traunecker, Claude. "L'Étoile diaconale copte et ses antécédents," *Cahiers de la Bibliothèque Copte* 3 (1986): 93–110.

———. *Coptos: hommes et dieux sur le parvis de Geb,* Orientalia Lovaniensa Analecta 63 (Leuven: Peeters, 1992).

Traunecker, Claude, Françoise Le Saout, and Olivier Masson, *La Chapelle d'Achôris à Karnak* 2, Mémoires du Centre franco-égyptien d'Étude des Temples de Karnak 2, Recherche sur les grandes civilizations 5 (Paris: Éditions ADPF, 1981).

Troy, Lana. *Patterns of Queenship in Ancient Egyptian Myth and History,* Boreas 14 (Uppsala: Liber Tryck AB, 1986).

Tylor, J.J., and Francis Ll. Griffith, *The Tomb of Paheri* (bound with Edouard Naville and T. Hayter Lewis, *Ahnas el Medineh*), EEF Memoir 11 (London: Egypt Exploration Fund, 1894).

Ullmann, Walter. *Medieval Political Thought* (Harmondsworth: Penguin, 1975).

van den Boorn, G.P.F. *The Duties of the Vizier, Civil Administration in the Early New Kingdom* (London and New York: Kegan Paul International, 1988).

Vandersleyen, Claude. *L'Égypte et la vallée du Nil* Tome 2: *de la fin de l'Ancien Empire à la fin du Nouvel Empire* (Paris: Presses Universitaires de France, 1995).

Vandier, J. *Moʿalla: La tombe d'Ankhtifi et la tombe de Sébekhotep,* BdÉ 18 (Cairo: Institut Français d'Archéologie Orientale, 1950).

Vercoutter, Jean. "New Egyptian Texts from the Sudan," *Kush* 4 (1956): 66–82.

———. "The Gold of Kush, Two Gold Washing Stations at Faras East," *Kush* 7 (1959): 120–53.

Verhoeven, Ursula. *Untersuchungen zur späthieratischen Buchschrift,* Orientalia Lovaniensa Analecta 99 (Leuven: Peeters, 2001).

Verhoeven, Ursula, and Philippe Derchain, *Le voyage de la déesse libyque: ein Text aus dem «Mutritual» des Pap. Berlin 3053,* Rites Égyptiens 5 (Brussels: Fondation Égyptologique Reine Élisabeth, 1985).

Vernus, Pascal. "Inscriptions de la troisième période intermédiaire (I)," *BIFAO* 75 (1975): 1–66.

———. "Littérature et autobiographie: les inscriptions de *Sꜣ-Mwt* surnommé *Kyky*," *RdÉ* 30 (1978): 115–46.

———. "Amun *Pꜣ-ʿḏr*: De la piété «populaire» à la spéculation théologique," in Jean Vercoutter, ed., *Hommages à la mémoire de Serge Sauneron, 1927–1976* 1: *Égypte pharaonique,* BdÉ 81 (Cairo, 1979), pp. 463–76.

———. "Études de philologie et de linguistique (IV)," *RdÉ* 36 (1985): 253–68.

Vikentiev, Vladimir. *La Haute crue du Nil et l'averse de l'an 6 du roi Taharqa; le dieu "Hemen" et son chef-lieu "Hefat",* Université Égyptienne Recueil de Travaux 4 (Cairo: Institut Français d'Archéologie Orientale, 1930).

von der Way, Thomas. *Göttergericht und "heiliger" Krieg im alten Ägypten: die Inschriften des Merenptah zum Libyerkrieg des Jahres 5,* SAGA 4 (Heidelberg: Heidelberger Orientverlag, 1992).

Vycichl, Werner. *Dictionnaire étymologique de la langue copte* (Leuven: Peeters, 1984).

Waddington, George, and Barnard Hanbury. *Journal of a Visit to Some Parts of Ethiopia* (London: John Murray, 1822).

Welsby, Derek A. *The Kingdom of Kush* (London: British Museum Press, 1996).

Welsby, Derek A., and Vivian Davies, eds., *Uncovering Ancient Sudan, a Decade of Discovery by the Sudan Archaeological Research Society,* Sudan Archaeological Research Society Publication Number 8 (London: Sudan Archaeological Research Society, 2002).

Welsby, Derek A., Mark G. Macklin, and Jamie C. Woodward, "Human Responses to Holocene Environmental Changes in the Northern Dongola Reach of the Nile, Sudan," in R. Friedman, ed., *Egypt and Nubia: Gifts of the Desert* (London: British Museum Press, 2002), pp. 28–38.

Wente, Edward F. "The Late Egyptian Conjunctive as a Past Continuative," *JNES* 21 (1962): 304–11.

———. "The Suppression of the High Priest Amenhotep," *JNES* 25 (1966): 73–87.

———. *Late Ramesside Letters,* SAOC 33 (Chicago: University of Chicago Press, 1967).

———. Review of Frandsen, *Outline of the Late Egyptian Verbal System,* in *JNES* 36 (1977): 310–12.

———. *Letters from Ancient Egypt,* Society of Biblical Literature, Writings from the Ancient World 1 (Atlanta: Scholars, 1990).

Westendorf, Wolfhart. *Koptisches Handwörterbuch* (Heidelberg: Carl Winter Universitätsverlag, 1965–1977).

Wiener, Malcolm H., and James P. Allen, "Separate Lives: The Ahmose Tempest Stela and the Theran Eruption," *JNES* 57 (1998): 1–28.

Wiesmann, H. "ⲙⲛⲧⲁϥ ⲉⲥⲱⲧⲙ er kann nicht hören," *ZÄS* 62 (1927): 66.

Wildung, Dietrich. "Queen Tiye Wearing a Hathor Headdress," in R. Freed, Y.J. Markowitz, and S.H. D'Auria, eds., *Pharaohs of the Sun: Akhenaton, Nefertiti, Tutankhamun* (Boston: Museum of Fine Arts, 1999), p. 215 (no. 39).

Williams, Bruce Beyer. *Twenty-Fifth Dynasty and Napatan Remains at Qustul: Cemeteries W and V,* Oriental Institute Nubian Expedition 7 (Chicago: The Oriental Institute of the University of Chicago, 1990).

———. "Serra East and the Mission of Middle Kingdom Fortresses in Nubia," in Emily Teeter and John A. Larson, eds., *Gold of Praise, Studies on Ancient Egypt in Honor of Edward F. Wente,* SAOC 58 (Chicago: The Oriental Institute of the University of Chicago, 1999), pp. 435–53.

Wilson, John A. "Ceremonial Games of the New Kingdom," *JEA* 17 (1931): 211–20.

Wilson, Penelope. *A Ptolemaic Lexikon, a Lexicographical Study of the Texts in the Temple of Edfu,* Orientalia Lovaniensa Analecta 78 (Leuven: Peeters, 1997).

Wimmer, Stefan. *Hieratische Paläographie der nicht-literarischen Ostraka der 19. und 20. Dynastie,* 2 vols., ÄAT 28 (Wiesbaden: Harrassowitz, 1995).

Winand, Jean. "L'expression du sujet nominal," *CdE* 63 (1989): 166–71.

———. *Études de néo-égyptien* 1: *la morphologie verbale,* Aegyptiaca Lealiensia 2 (Liège: Centre Informatique de Philologie et Letters, 1992).

———. "À la croisée du temps, de l'aspect et du mode: le conjonctif en néo-égyptien," *Lingua Aegyptia* 9 (2001): 293–329.

Winand, Jean. "Les décrets oraculaires pris en l'honneur d'Henouttaouy et de Maâtkarê (Xe et VIIe Pylônes)," *Cahiers de Karnak* 11, fasc. 2 (Paris: Éditions Recherche sur les Civilisations, 2003), pp. 603–711.

Yellin, Janice W. "Egyptian Religion and its ongoing Impact on the Formation of the Napatan State: a Contribution to László Török's Main Paper: The Emergence of the Kingdom of Kush and her Myth of the State in the First Millennium BC," *CRIPEL* 17/1 (1995): 243–63.

Zabkar, Louis. *Hymns to Isis in her Temple at Philae* (Hanover: University Press of New England, 1988).

Zauzich, Karl-Theodor. "Das Lamm des Bokchoris," in *Festschrift zum 100-jährigen Bestehen der Papyrussammlung der Österreichischen Nationalbibliothek, Papyrus Erzhog Rainer (P. Rainer Cent.)* (Vienna: Brüder Hollinek, 1983), pp. 165–74 and pl. 2.

Zibelius-Chen, Karola. "Überlegungen zur ägyptischen Nubienpolitik in der Dritten Zwischenzeit," *SAK* 16 (1989): 329–45.

———. "Das nachkoloniale Nubien: politische Fragen der Entstehung des kuschitischen Reiches," in Rolf Gundlach, Manfred Kropp, and Annalis Leibundgut, eds., *Der Sudan in Vergangenheit und Gegenwart,* Nordostafrikanisch-westasiatische Studien 1 (Frankfurt: Peter Lang, 1996), pp. 195–217.

———. "Die Kubanstele Ramses' II. und die nubischen Goldregionen," in C. Berger, G. Clerc, and N. Grimal, eds., *Hommages à Jean Leclant* 2: *Nubie, Soudan, Éthiopie,* BdÉ 106/2 (Cairo: Institut Français d'Archéologie Orientale, 1994), pp. 411–17.

Zivie-Coche, Christiane. *Giza au premier millénaire, autour du temple d'Isis Dame des Pyramides* (Boston: Museum of Fine Arts, 1991).

Glossary

The glossary to Katimala's Semna tableau includes words in the annotations to the scene (labeled l. A + line number), and ll. 1-11 of the main inscription (labeled simply as l. + line number).

General Vocabulary

i

i	first person singular suffix pronoun, l. 2 (three times unwritten); l. 3 (five times); l. 4 (five times, once unwritten); l. 5 (unwritten); l. 6 (thrice, twice unwritten); l. 9; l. A2 (unwritten)
iꜣy	particle, l. 4
iꜣd	verb, "to attack," l. 3
iw	particle, l. 1 (twice), l. 2 (six times); l. 3; l. 4; l. 6; l. 7 (twice); l. 8 (twice); l. 9, l. 10 (thrice)
iwnꜣ	enclitic negator, l. 8
im(*i*)	verb, imperative of *rḏi*, "to give, cause," l. A7
in	preposition, "by" (or element in the *sḏm.in=f* form), l. 1; l. A1
ir	particle, l. 6; l. 8
ir.t	noun, "eye," l. A1
iri	verb, "to do, make, treat," l. 2; l. 3 (twice); l. 4 (twice); l. 6 (thrice); l. 7 (thrice); l. 8 (seven times); l. 9 (restored); l. 10; l. 11 (twice)
irm	preposition, "together with, and," l. 5; l. 6 (partly restored)
isṯ	particle, l. 5 (written *is.tw*); l. 8; l. 9
it	noun, "father," l. 4; l. 5 (partly restored); l. 6; l. 9

ꜥ

ꜥwꜣi͗	verb, "to rob," l. 2; l. 3
ꜥm	verb, "to swallow, absorb, understand," l. 4; l. 7 (twice)
ꜥnḫ	verb, "to live," l. 7; l. 8 (twice)
ꜥnḫ	noun, "life," l. A9
ꜥḏꜣ	adjective, "false," l. 8
ꜥḏn	noun, "destruction," l. 10

w

w	third person plural suffix pronoun, l. 2; l. 4; l. 6 (four times); l. 8 (twice, once restored)

w (continued)

wywy	verb, "to be reluctant or unable; to be inept, disabled" (for *wiꜣwiꜣ*), l. 4 (written *wy—sp-sn*)
wꜥꜣ	verb and noun, "to curse," l. 2
wnn	verb, "to be, exist," l. 1 (in *iw wn*); l. 2 (in *iw wn*); l. 5; l. 6 (twice)
wr	noun, "chieftain, great one," l. 2; l. 5
wr.t	feminine adjective, "great," l. 1 (in title *ḥm.t-nsw.t wr.t*); l. A3 (in title *ḥm.t-nsw.t wr.t*); l. A6 (in title *ḥm.t-nswt wr.t*); l. A8 (in title *ḥm.t-nswt wr.t*)

b

bꜣk	verb, "to work, serve," l. 1
bꜣk	noun, "servant," l. 1; l. 3
bin	adjective, "bad, evil," l. 2 (used adverbially); l. 5; l. 7 (four times); l. 8; l. 9; ll. 10-11; l. 11
bity	see *nswt-bity*
bw	negative particle, l. 7
bw-pw	conjugation base of the negative preterite, l. 3; l. 10
bn	negative particle, l. 1; l. 8

p

pꜣ	masculine singular definite article, l. 3 (twice); l. 4; l. 5 (twice); l. 7 (twice); l. 8 (twice); l. 9 (twice); l. 11 (four times)
Pr-ꜥꜣ	noun, "palace, pharaoh," l. 5
Pr.t	noun, "Peret Season," l. 1
pḥ.wy	noun, "hind-quarters, back," l. 5
pḥrr	verb "to run," l. 11 (twice)
ptr	particle, l. 7; l. 8 (partly restored)

f

f	3rd person masculine singular suffix pronoun, l. 1, l. 2 (twice); l. 4 (twice); l. 5; l. 6; l. 7 (four times); l. 8; l. 10 (twice); l. 11 (thrice)

m

m	preposition, "in, from" (in the compound preposition *m-ẖnw*), l. 1; l. 2 (written *n*); l. 3 (three times, once as status pronominalis *im*, once in compound *m-ḏr*); l. 4 (thrice, once in compund *m-ḫt*); l. 5; l. 7 (four times, twice in compound *m-di*, once as status pronominalis *im*); l. 9 (twice, once written *n*); l. 10
mꜣꜥ.ti-ḫrw	epithet, "justifid, vindicated" (of living person), l. 1; l. A5 (restored); l. A7
mi	preposition, "like," l. 5; l. 9; l. 10; l. 11
my	particle, l. 7 (partly restored)
mw.t	noun, "mother," l. A1
mn	negative particle, l. 2 (three times)
mn.t	noun, "daytime," l. 9; l. 10

***m** (continued)*

mšʿ	noun, "army, force," l. 11
mtw	conjugation base of the conjunctive, l. 2
md.t	noun, "matter," l. 2; l. 3; l. 6

n

n	preposition, "to, for," l. 1; l. 2; l. 3; l. 4 (twice); l. 6; l. 7; l. 8; l. 10; l. 11 (twice)
n	indirect genitive, l. 1 (for plural); l. 2; l. 3; l. 5 (twice, once uncertain for plural); l. 9 (twice); l. 10 (twice); l. A3; l. A9
n	first person plural suffix pronoun, l. 2 (twice); l. 7
nꜣ	plural definite article, l. 1; l. 6; l. 10
nꜣy	plural possessive adjective, l. 4; l. 5; l. 6 (twice, once restored); l. 9
niw.t	noun, "city," l. 10
ny-sw	possessive construction (adjectival use of genitival *n* + dependent pronoun), l. 9
nb	adjective, "all, every," l. 6; l. 10; l. A2
nbw	noun, "gold," l. 2; l. 3; l. 4
nfr	adjective verb, "good," l. 5; l. 6; l. 7; l. 8; l. 9
nfr	noun, "good, goodness," l. 8 (twice); l. 11
nḫt	adjective verb, "strong, powerful, victorious," l. 4
nswt	noun, "king," l. 1; l. A3 (twice); l. A6 (twice); l. A8 (twice, once in title *ḥm.t-nswt wr.t)*
nsw.t-bity	noun, "dual king," l. A8
nty	masculine singular relative adjective, l. 7 (twice, once partly restored); l. 8; l. 11 (twice, once partly restored)
nṯr	noun, "god," l. 4; l. 8 (partly restored); l. A1; l. A2

r

r	preposition, "to, against," l. 2 (twice; once written *rr=*, once written *irr=*, both in *status pronominalis*); l. 3; l. 5 (in the compound *r-ḥꜣ.t*); l. 6 (*ir=* in *status pronominalis*); l. 7; l. 11 (twice in the compound *r-ḥꜣ.t*)
rwi	verb, "to flee," l. 3 (partly restored)
rmṯ	noun, "people," l. 10
rnp.t	noun, "year," l. 2; l. 3; l. 4; l. 6
rḫy(.t)	noun, "people," l. 7
rḏi	verb, "to give, cause," l. 2 (three times, in ⲧⲁⲣⲉϥⲥⲱⲧⲙ finalis); l. 4; l. 7

h

hy	noun, "annals," l. 9
hnn	verb, "to lean on, trust," l. 3
hrw	noun, "day," l. 9

ḥ

ḥꜣ.t	noun, "forepart," in compound preposition *r-ḥꜣ.t*, "in front of, before," l. 5; l. 11 (twice)

***ḥ* (continued)**

ḥ3	preposition, "surrounding," l. A9
ḥm	noun, "majesty," l. 1
ḥm.t	noun, "wife," l. 1 (in title *ḥm.t-nsw.t wrt*); l. 6; l. A3 (in title *ḥm.t-nswt wr.t*); l. A6 (in title *ḥm.t-nswt wr.t*); l. A8 (in title *ḥm.t-nswt wr.t*)
ḥmsi	verb, "to sit, dwell," l. 6
ḥnw.t	noun, "mistress," l. A2
ḥr	preposition, "upon, because of," l. 6
ḥsb.t	noun, "regnal year," l. 1
ḥk3	noun, "magic," l. 4
ḥḏ	noun, "silver," l. 2; l. 3

ḫ

ḫ3ʿ	verb, "to throw, abandon," l. 5
ḫpr	verb, "to occur," l. 2 (four times, once as participle *iḫpr*); l. 3 (as participle *iḫpr*); l. 6
ḫpš	noun, "forearm, strong arm," l. 5
ḫfty	noun, "enemy," l. 2; l. 3
ḫr	proclitic particle, l. 4 (twice); l. 6 (twice); l. 8 (twice)
ḫrwy	noun, "enemy," l. 5; l. 6
ḫrp	verb, "to control, drive," l. 9
ḫrp(.t)	noun, "herd," l. 9 (twice)
ḫt	preposition, "through, throughout," l. 4 (in the compound *m-ḫt*)

ẖ

ẖnw	preposition, "in" (in the compound preposition *m-ẖnw*), l. 1

s

s	third person singular feminine suffix pronoun (written *sw*), l. 2; l. A9
s.t	noun, "place," l. 8 (twice)
s3.t-nsw.t	compound noun, "daughter of the king," l. 1; l. A3; l. A6
s3	noun, "protection," l. A9
sin	verb, "to hasten," l. 4
snḏ	verb, "to fear," l. 5
sḥwr	verb, "to curse," l. 10
sḥtp	noun, "bouquet," l. A3; l. A7
sḫ3	verb, "to recall, remember," l. 3
ssnḏ	causative verb, "to frighten," l. 6

š

š3ʿ	preposition, l. 8
šʿ.t	noun, "slaughter," l. 9
šsp	verb, "to receive, to succeed," l. 4; ll. 5-6; l. A2; l. A7

ḳ

ḳḳ	verb, "to strip," l. 5
ḳd	noun, "form, character, nature, disposition," l. 5; l. 9; l. 10; l. 11

k

k.t	noun, "another (feminine)," l. 8
kꜣyw	noun, "others (plural)," l. 8

t

tꜣ	feminine singular definite article, l. 2 (twice); l. 3 (twice); l. 4; l. 6 (twice); l. 9 (twice, once written *tꜣy*)
tꜣy	feminine sing. possessive adjective, l. 8
tꜣ	noun, "land, earth," l. 8; l. 11
twnn	1st person plural proclitic pronoun, l. 1 (twice)
tnw	interrogative adverb, "where," l. 1

ṯ

ṯni	verb, "to distinguish, exault," l. 3

d

di	preposition, in compound *m-di*, l. 7 (twice)
dmi	verb, "to touch, accrue, befall," l. 10

ḏ

ḏw	noun, "mountain," l. 4
ḏr	preposition, "since, when," in compound *m-ḏr*, l. 3
ḏrw	noun, "end, limit," l. 11
ḏd	verb, "to say, speak," l. 1; l. 4; l. 8; l. A1

Numbers

2	l. 1
9	l. 1
14	l. 1
30	l. 5

Personal Names

Mkꜣrš	Makaresh, ll. 9–10; l. 10
Kꜣtimꜣlw	Katimala, l. 1; ll. A4–5 (partly restored); ll. A6–7

Divine Names

ꜣs.t	Isis, l. A1
Imn	Amun, l. 2; l. 3 (twice); l. 8 (twice); l. 9 (twice)
Rꜥ	Re, l. A2

Grammatical Index

As with the glossary, the grammatical index includes words in the annotations to the scene (labeled l. A + line number), and ll. 1–11 of the main inscription (labeled simply as l. + line number).

Non-Verbal Sentences

Adjectival sentence	l. 4; l. 5 (twice); l. 7 (twice); l. 8 (thrice); l. 9 (twice); ll. 10–11; l. 11
Circumstantialized	l. 9
Adverbial sentence	l. 1
Cleft sentence	l. 3
Existential sentence	ll. 1–2; l. 2
One-membral nominal sentence	
Circumstantial Negative	l. 8

Sentence Conjugation

First Present	l. 3; l. 4
Circumstantial	l. 4; l. 6; l. 8; see also virtual relative
Circumstantial Negative	l. 1
Relativized with *wn*	ll. 5–6; l. 6
Relativized with *nty*	l. 7; l. 8; l. 11
with Preterite Converter	l. 6
ⲧⲁⲣⲉϥⲥⲱⲧⲙ̄ Finalis	
Circumstantial Negative	l. 2 (thrice)
Third Future	l. 7

Clause Conjugation

Conjunctive	l. 2
Temporal	l. 3

Suffix Conjugation

Negative Aorist	
Relativized with *nty*	l. 7

Index

Plates

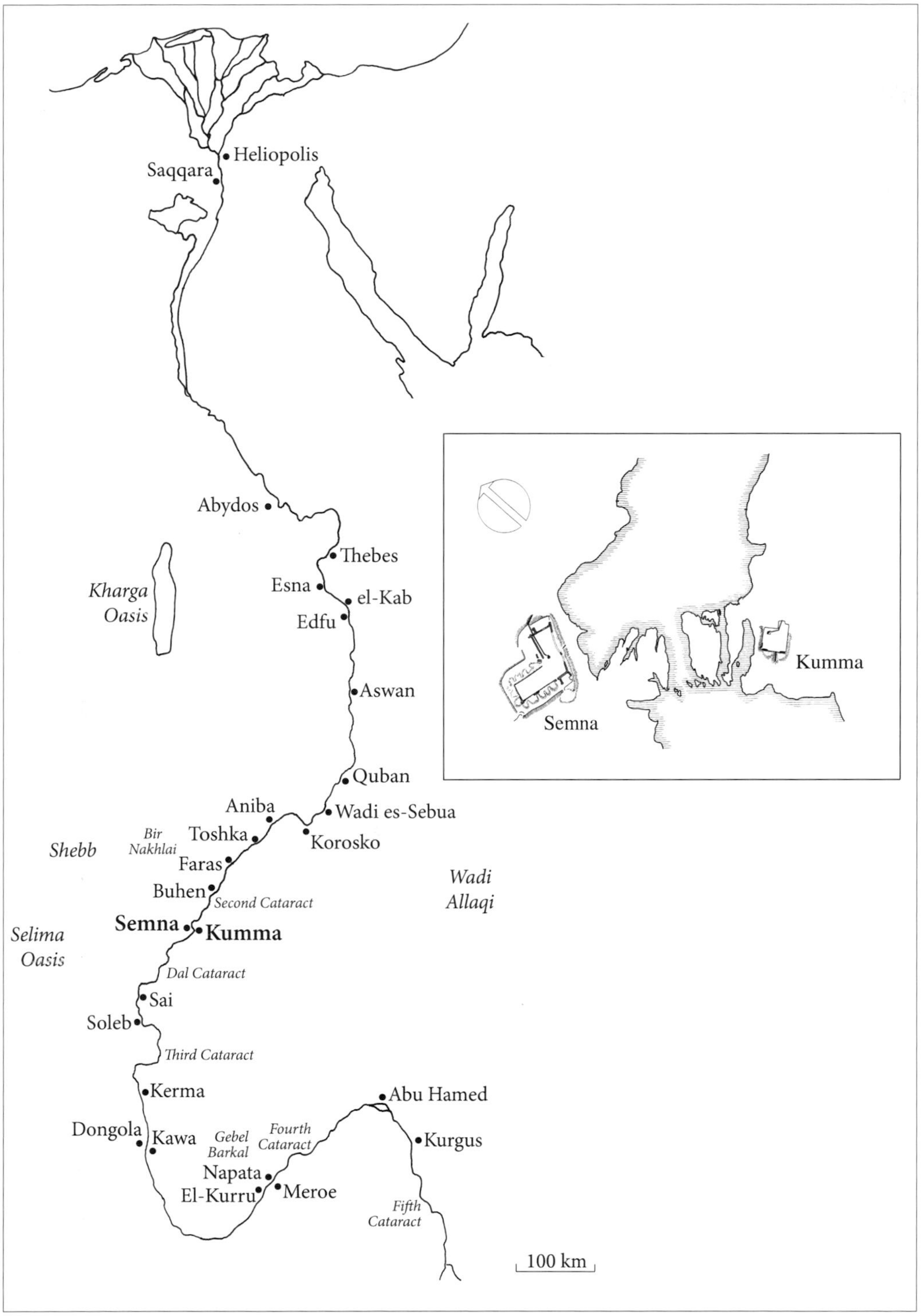

Pl. 1 *Map of Egypt and Nubia, showing the location of Semna Temple (insert detail after Keating,* Nubian Rescue, *p. 124).*

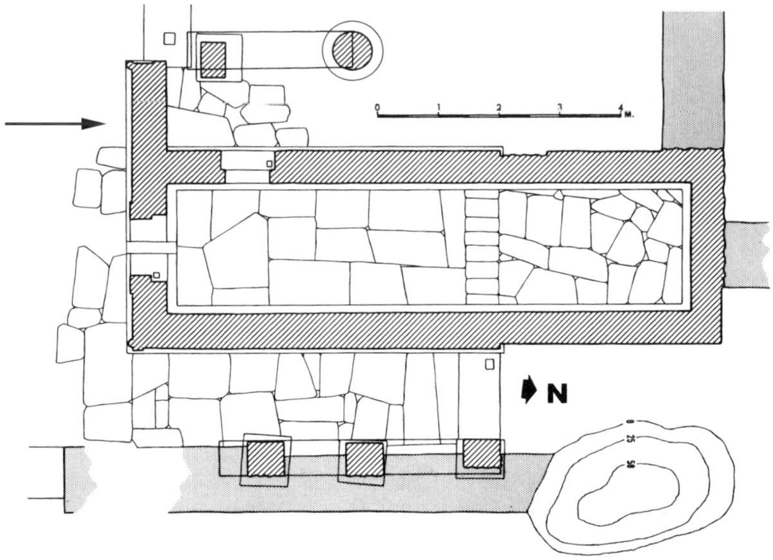

PL. II.A *Plan of the Temple of Semna showing the Location of the Tableau of Katimala (after Caminos,* Semna-Kumma *I, pl. 3).*

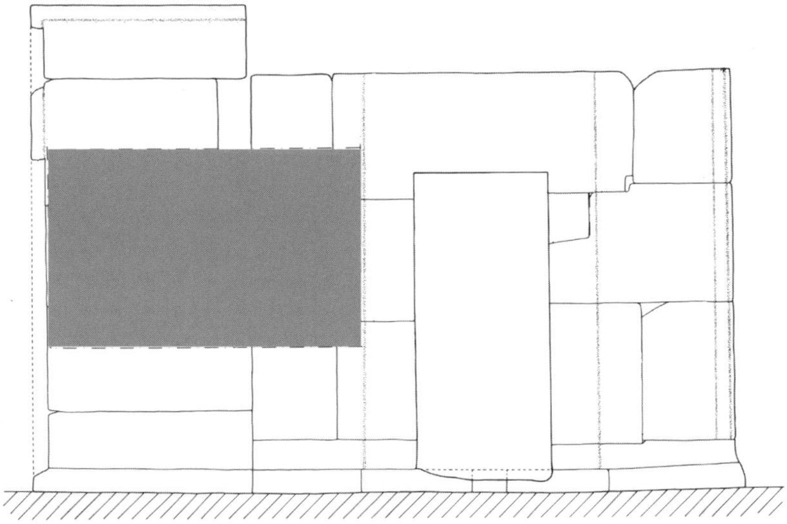

PL. II.B *Elevation of the South Wall; Katimala Inscription shaded (after Caminos,* Semna-Kumma *I, pl. 7).*

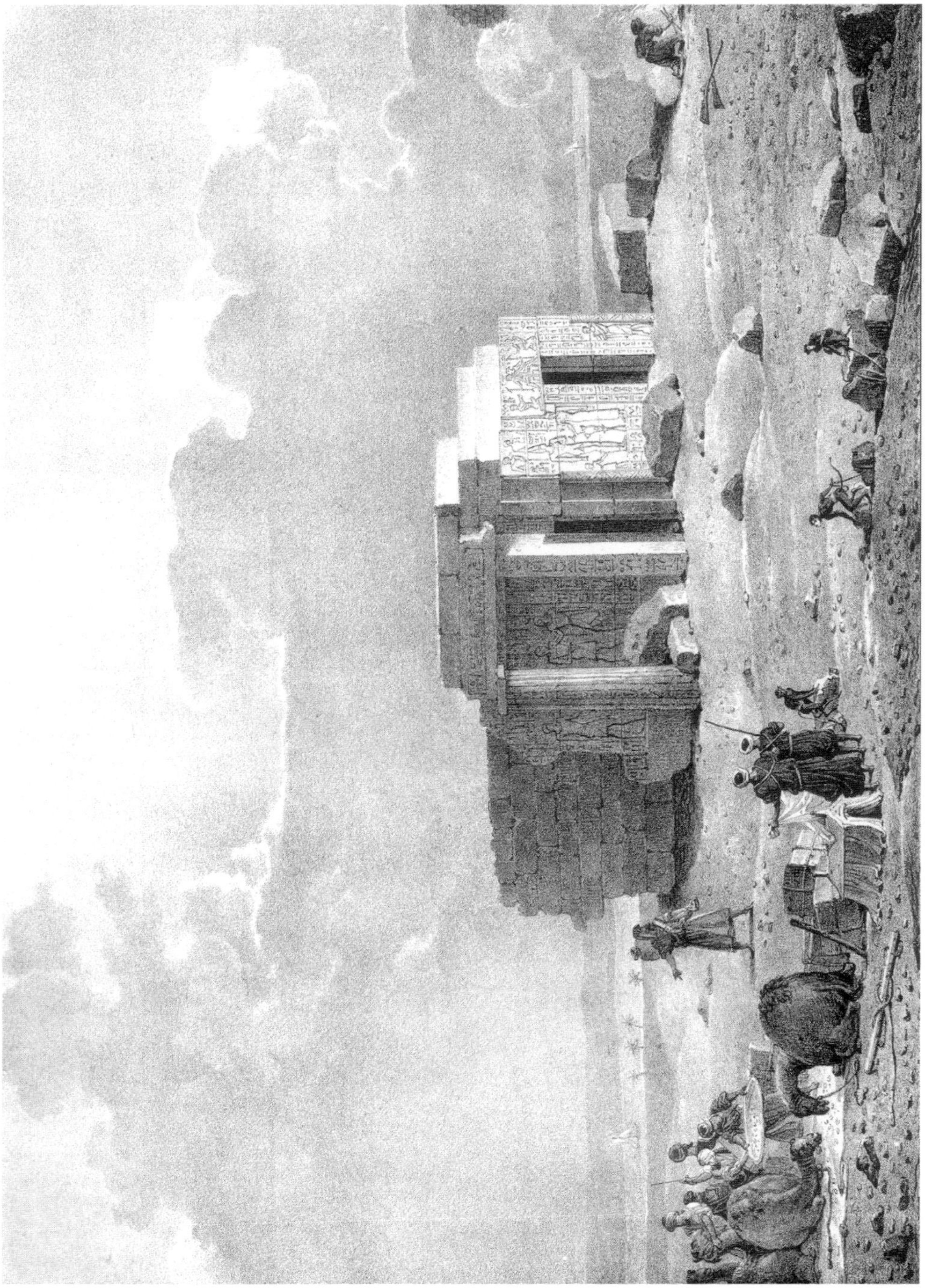

PL. III *The Temple of Semna, with the Katimala tableau visible (from Cailliaud,* Voyage à Méroé, *pl.24).*

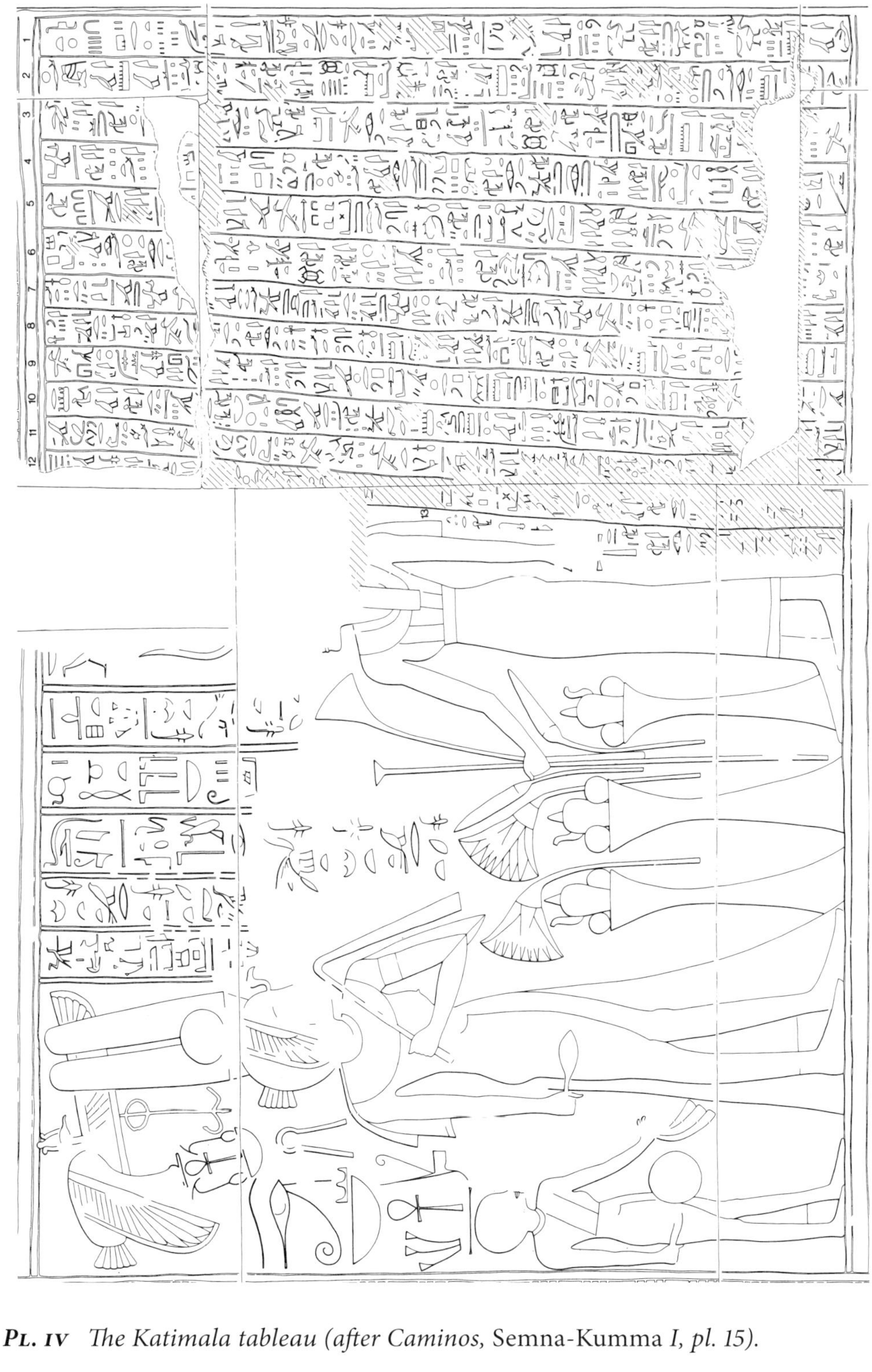

Pl. iv *The Katimala tableau (after Caminos,* Semna-Kumma *I, pl. 15).*

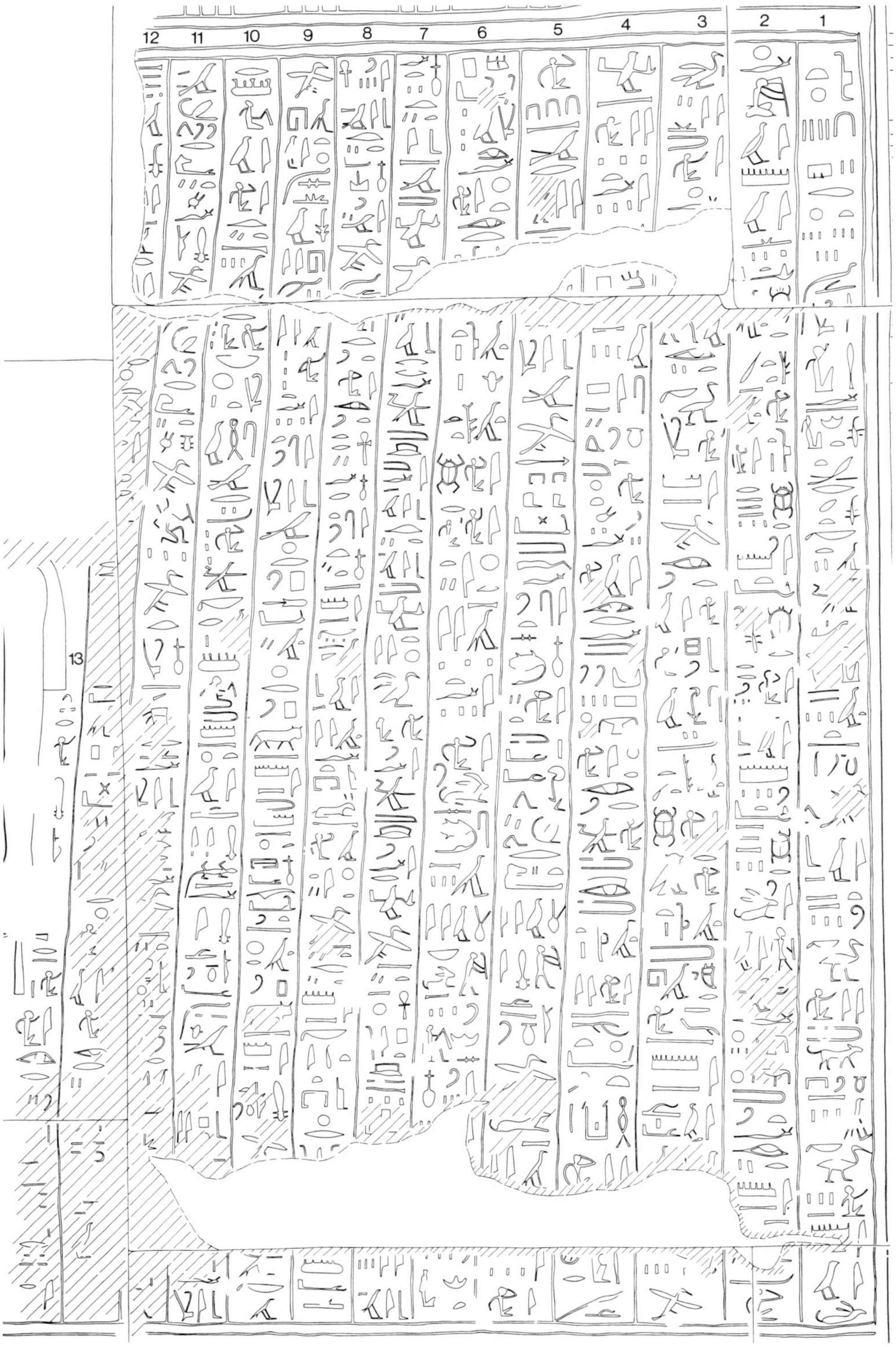

Pl. v *Detail of the main inscription of Katimala (after Caminos,* Semna-Kumma *I, pl. 17).*

PL. VI *Hieroglyphic transcription of the main inscription of Katimala.*

Pl. vii *The Katimala tableau (Photograph courtesy of The Oriental Institute of the University of Chicago).*

PL. VIII *Detail of the main inscription of Katimala (Photograph courtesy of The Oriental Institute of the University of Chicago).*